WITHDRAWN

FV

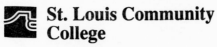

CHINA AND ITS NATIONAL MINORITIES

Autonomy or Assimilation?

CHINA AND ITS NATIONAL MINORITIES

Autonomy or Assimilation?

THOMAS HEBERER

An East Gate Book

M. E. Sharpe, Inc.
ARMONK, NEW YORK
LONDON, ENGLAND

An East Gate Book

Available in the United Kingdom and Europe from M. E. Sharpe, Publishers, 3 Henrietta Street, London WC2E 8LU.

Translation by Michel Vale.

Library of Congress Cataloging-in-Publication Data

Heberer, Thomas.
    [Nationalitätenpolitik und Entwicklungspolitik in den Gebieten nationaler Minderheiten in China. English]
    China and its national minorities: autonomy or assimilation? / by Thomas Heberer.
        p.   cm.
    Rev. translation of: Nationalitätenpolitik und Entwicklungspolitik in den Gebieten nationaler Minderheiten in China.
    Includes index.
    ISBN 0-87332-549-4
    1. Ethnology—China. 2. China—Ethnic relations. I. Title.
DS730.H4213   1989
305.8′00951—dc19   88-38363
                                                CIP

Printed in the United States of America

BB   10 9 8 7 6 5 4 3 2 1

To Franziska and Georg Heberer and
Jing and Feng Mei

Contents

Illustrations

Tables

Preface

This book owes its origins to the wish to make my study *Nationalitäten-politik und Entwicklungspolitik in den Gebieten nationaler Minderheiten in China* (Nationality Policy and Development Policy in Ethnic Minority Regions in China) accessible to English-speaking readers. That original study was published by the University of Bremen in 1984 in two parts: a general section on the development of nationality policy, and a special section dealing with the Yi in the Liangshan Autonomous Prefecture (Sichuan Province). The second part was based on material gathered during an extensive research visit to several counties of this prefecture in the summer of 1981. Since the vastness of the project proved to be prohibitive to the production of an English edition, however, the author and M. E. Sharpe, Inc. agreed instead to publish a volume on some of the current and key problems of the nationality question in China. This meant that most of the material on the Yi had to be dropped from this edition; it is available to the interested reader in the above-mentioned book which, however, is available only in German.

CHINA AND ITS NATIONAL MINORITIES

Autonomy or Assimilation?

1

Introduction to the Problem

Conflicts between majorities and minorities, between the nationalities within a country, and between those in different countries, are worldwide phenomena that are causing a resurgence in the study of nationality problems in the social sciences. The problems of ethnic minorities and their inherent potentials for conflict are themselves important factors in the numerous international conflicts that take place against the backdrop of national conflicts. Since national minorities can be used or exploited for or against a country's interests, in multinational states the stability of a country quite often depends on the system of relations woven among its different peoples.

This study, which is concerned specifically with China, belongs in that general classification of works dealing with the analysis and documentation of minority problems. Accordingly, it will be useful first to illuminate the global character of the nationality problem on the basis of a few examples. The definition of a few terms (general terms as well as specifically Chinese terminology) will help to give a better picture of the nuances of the minority question, with special reference to the Chinese situation.

The nationality question in an international context

Nationality problems and conflicts exist today in most countries. Whereas larger ethnic minorities are often able to defend themselves politically and, not infrequently, militarily against oppression, exploitation, and assimilation, the minor nationalities (such as the Indians of South America) are often exterminated, their cultures destroyed, their lands confiscated, and their strength sapped by disease, hunger, persecution, and illiteracy.[1] According to UN estimates, 200 million hunters and gatherers are today faced with annihilation through hunger, disease, and war. And not only do the governments of the native countries contribute to this annihilation, but so also do the multinational concerns and local Christian missions.[2] This is equally true of developed countries—such as the United States, the Soviet Union, Canada, Australia, New Zealand—and Third World countries.

For example, in North America, and in most of the South and Central American countries in which the Indian population makes up less than 5 percent of the total population, Indians live on reservations as a national minority, often with restricted rights. In Brazil, for example, according to the "law for Indians," Indians are regarded as legally nonresponsible, and are therefore subject to Brazilian guardianship law.[3]

Historically, Indian peoples have been violently exterminated in the Americas when they have stood in the way of the extraction of raw materials, construction of highways, or other projects.[4] It is no different on other continents. For example,

> In 1967 the Australian aborigines solemnly obtained their civil rights in their own country—and in addition access to alcohol—under UN pressure. For them, alcohol has become a status symbol of equality with the whites. Since then, more and more of them are to be found hanging about in a drunken stupor on the outskirts of cities. They are losing all points of reference to the world about them, and have proved unable to cope with the other "gifts" of the white man, namely tuberculosis, measles, prostitution, venereal diseases, and money, competitiveness, and greed. Thus the aborigines, invested with their "civil rights," are now threatened by degeneration, the total forgetting of the skills that were necessary for survival, and indeed, a loss of instinct pure and simple. Unable to adapt to that which has never before occurred, to the new, to the unintelligible, to the never practiced, these vestigial Stone Age groups are suspended between two worlds, and their creative capacities are stifled and paralyzed. They opt for resignation and so are lost.[5]

The Kurds were dispersed arbitrarily into several countries, where they have been subject to severe persecution and cultural oppression.[6] More than 150,000 Papuans have been killed since 1967 when the Suharto regime took power.[7] The gypsies, who have lived for more than a century in the Netherlands, have neither the right to determine their own lifestyle nor guarantees that they may remain permanently in that country.[8] The Maori of New Zealand and the aborigines of Australia had their land violently taken from them on a mass scale.[9] And the Federal Republic of Germany has its own nationality problem of gypsies and foreign workers; the federal government has yet to make full restitution for the crimes committed against them during the the National Socialist (Nazi) era. The litany goes on and on.

In the Soviet Union, the thesis of the "convergence and fusion of the nations under socialism" produced a policy of denationalization, putting the non-Russian nationalities under heavy pressure. The principle means used were:

—providing moral, political, material, and economic advantages to the Russified while discriminating against nationality-conscious non-Russians;

—the "internationalization" of national cultures through the administratively forced spread of the Russian language; and

—an "international exchange of cadres" and migration of Russians, with "internationalization" usually meaning "Russification."[10]

Just recently, the Soviet nationalities have started to fight openly for their national rights, leading the Soviet Union into a new phase of awakening nationalities consciousness.

In the late seventies, Karoly Kiraly, a top-level Rumanian Communist Party official of Hungarian origin, wrote to the Bucharest party leadership that the "tendency to force the assimilation of the national minorities living in Rumania is obvious and undeniable."[11] In Hungary, the gypsies have not been recognized as an independent nationality since 1961 and are therefore also subject to the threat of forced assimilation.[12]

Major nationality problems also exist for China's Asian neighbors. In Burma, the Shan and Karens have been carrying on a struggle for autonomy for years. The Burmese government, which has engaged itself militarily against these peoples, has refused them this right.[13] The situation is not much different among the mountain tribes in Thailand, who are often held by opium traders in a state of slave-like dependence.[14] The mountain tribes were not granted Thai citizenship until 1974; previously they were regarded as Communists or "aliens."[15] India, the country with the greatest number of ethnic minorities, has deprived its minorities of their means of subsistence by confiscating their land and expelling them, and essentially threatening them with extinction.[16] The resistance of the mountain people in Laos and Vietnam to resettlement projects is combated by military means, including the use of napalm and poison gas.[17] The minorities in the Philippines, i.e., those who do not belong to the dominant Malaysian race, have had their living space constricted and are continually engaged in bloody skirmishes with government troops.[18] And in Indonesia where there are about 30 different ethnic groups, only "Indonesians," no national minorities, exist officially.[19] "Bahasa Indonesia" (the Indonesian language) has been the official language and the language of instruction in the schools since independence, and cultural autonomy is suppressed.[20]

These examples are graphic evidence that ethnic minorities are subjected to discrimination, oppression, and persecution in the East and West as well as in third-world countries, and that so far not even the beginning of a solution has been found to the minority problem.

There was only sparse information in the sixties and seventies on minorities in China and their actual situation. Official Chinese comments were usually stereotyped: "the working peoples of the different nationalities have become masters of their land and have achieved total political emancipation,"[21] or "all the nationalities of China are united as never before."[22] Problems were rarely even alluded to in official descriptions. Since very little material was available and the Chinese authorities painted a picture of "unison and harmony," the impression was orchestrated that China was conducting an exemplary nationality policy.[23]

However, since 1978 the Chinese leadership has openly admitted that there were very few changes, if any, in the conditions in minority regions for quite some time and down to the late seventies, and that during the Cultural Revolution there were incidents of violent devastation and severe oppression in minority regions. The consequences were not only chronic economic and cultural backwardness but also a large measure of alienation between the Han (China's largest nationality, generally known as Chinese) and the ethnic minorities.

The concept of national minority

A closer examination of the term "national minority" shows that the nationality problem is much more complex than is evident from the above description. The term "minority" embraces a group of people who differ in a number of distinctive specific characteristics from the rest of the population of a country whose territory they inhabit. These characteristics may derive from race, language, religion, customs, morals, traditions, dress, social organization, etc. In any case they will be common to all the members of such a group, and make it relatively easy to distinguish them from other groups. Both objective factors, such as the specific relation between the minority and the majority, and subjective factors—say, the minority group's consciousness of itself—are involved in the definition of the term. "Minority" is primarily understood to be a group that does not share the ethnic or national characteristics of the majority of the population. The existence of different categories of minorities creates an additional difficulty in formulating a precise and comprehensive definition. Different types include:

1. *Autochthonous and immigrant groups.* A basic distinction must be drawn between groups whose territorial habitat is also the heartland of their culture (e.g., Tamils in India, aborigines in Australia, and Maoris in New Zealand) and those whose heartland (linguistically, culturally, and usually also politically) is located in another country to which they immigrated (e.g., Germans in the Soviet Union, Chinese in Southeast Asia), as well as to groups who were brought forcibly to another place (e.g., Negroes in the United States). Furthermore, it is necessary to distinguish between socioeconomically more developed peoples who have immigrated into areas of less developed peoples, and those who have acquired those areas through conquest and subsequently subjugated or expelled the autochthonous population (e.g., as did Europeans on the North American continent, in South Africa, in Australia, and in New Zealand), and immigration without conquest or subjugation (Chinese and Indians in Southeast Asia, Germans in Rumania).

2. *National, linguistic, and religious minorities.* Most national mi-

norities use a language that is different from that of the majority. But the particularity of language is not crucial to the designation "national minority." For instance, the Negroes in the United States or the Hui in China speak the same language as the majority population. Other groups may speak their own language without considering themselves a separate nationality and thus are only a linguistic, not a national minority (e.g., the Cantonese and the Hakka in China). There are also religious minorities who have been conceded the status of a nationality in certain countries on the basis of their particular cultural—although not necessarily racial or linguistic—development (e.g., the "Moslem" nationality group in Yugoslavia, and the Hui in China).

3. *Territorial minorities*. There are minority groups who inhabit a clear-cut territory (e.g., the Bretons in France, the Naga in India, the Buriats in the Soviet Union), and groups who live scattered over a vast area (Indians in East Africa; Jews and Rom throughout Europe). There are groups who live in border areas (Hungarians in Yugoslavia, Malaysians in Thailand, Kirgiz in China), and groups whose territory is an enclave within the territory of the majority population (various Indian groups in South America, the Yi and She in China).

4. *Socioeconomic development differentiations*. Different nationalities represent differing stages of development, although today the tendency is increasingly toward convergence. Minorities that numerically are quite large (such as the Ukrainians in the Soviet Union or the Erytrians in Ethiopia) and whose socioeconomic development is at a level with that of the majority are often a politically weightier factor than, say, marginal groups that are still at the "hunter and gatherer" stage and are numerically of minor importance.

5. *Political minorities*. The apartheid policy in South Africa, for instance, shows that a numerical minority (the whites) can quite easily constitute a political majority. In English, therefore, the term minority is also construed to mean "nondominant group." The minority will then be a political minority, although representing the majority of the population.

The complexity of defining minorities, as well as the complexity of the nationality question in general, should be evident from the above delineations.[24] This is compounded by the context in which the nationality question first arose in a particular country. Thus, (among other categories) there are:

—nationality-states that were formed over the course of history through the incorporation of several major nationalities and that have by and large forged relations of equality among the different nationalities (e.g., Switzerland, Yugoslavia);

—multiethnic states created by the territorial borders drawn by colonial powers without consideration for ethnic boundaries, and in which subgroups of different nationalities live (most of the countries of Africa);

—multiethnic states formed by the territorial expansion of the largest nationality, usually through conquests (Russia and China are examples of this type);

—multiethnic states in which immigrants in modern times have subjugated the autochthonous population and have thereby become the dominant ethnic group in the state (for example, Australia, North America, South Africa); and

—states that have become multinational states through peaceful immigration (as in Malaysia and Indonesia).

In western social sciences, "national minority" is generally construed to mean an ethnic group that is in principle an integral part of the larger society, but that does not actually "participate to an equal degree in the enjoyment of social goods as do the other members of that society."[25] The term could refer to situations in which "a portion of the state's population is permanently and decisively prevented from participating in the democratizing process and in the exercise of civil rights."[26] Real equality could be achieved only through the abandonment of ethnic distinctiveness, i.e., through assimilation.[27]

Discrimination or hostile tensions between minority and majority are thus declared to be a defining characteristic of a minority. But this definition, which has its origins in the conditions of the modern nation-states of Europe, seems to be correct neither extensionally or intentionally. It describes a national minority in purely negative terms and, moreover, as a group containing an internal contradiction that can only be resolved through the minority concerned abandoning its identity. It assumes *a priori* that the minority problem is basically insoluble without the elimination of the minority. The logical implication would be that the problem can ultimately be solved only through the assimilation of the minority, through expulsion, or by redrawing borders. A balanced coexistence and the equal participation of ethnic minorities as equals in the democratic process, the right of self-administration in the form of autonomy, and aid in socioeconomic development while still promoting the preservation of ethnic identity are thus all declared impossible. The above definition presumes that (a) most (but not all) ethnic minorities are to varying degrees oppressed or discriminated against by the nationality in control of the state; and (b) most minorities see themselves as objectively disadvantaged despite equal rights (thus their language cannot become an official language in the state, they are subject to alienation, or their special interests are only conditionally met). However, it does not necessarily follow from (b) that they are in fact discriminated against in every case, and that therefore all minorities are in roughly the same situation.

If we attempt to classify the minorities in China, we find that China is a multinational state formed from the territorial expansion of the largest nationality (Han) and from a fusion between the Han and different peoples over the course of history. The minorities in China today include autochthonous and immigrant groups, national and religious groups, groups living on a clearly circumscribed territory, as well as groups living dispersed over a large area, groups living in border regions, and groups constituting enclaves within the Han territory. There were (and still are) major differences as to the level of socioeconomic development as well: some of these minorities were still at the level of "primitive society," i.e., they were hunters and gatherers, while others were slave-holders, liege-lords, or following feudal structures. The differences required—and continue to require—a nationality policy that takes into account the distinctive features of each minority. This complex composition of Chinese minority groups thus calls for a more differentiated approach to the minority problem than that which would be adequate for studying countries with a less complex nationality structure.

Problems of definition

All ethnic groups that do not belong to the majority Han nationality in the People's Republic of China are today designated "national minorities" (*shaoshu minzu*). The policy pursued with these minorities and the terms used in defining that policy employ the reference word "nationalities" (*minzu*), as in nationality policy, nationality commis-

Table 1.1

Ethnic Minorities

According to 1982 population census				According to State Statistics Bureau*	
Zhuang	13,383,086	Daur	94,126	Total	85,927,000
Hui	7,228,398	Jingpo	92,976	Zhuang	16,150,000
Uygur	5,963,491	Mulam	90,357	Manchu	9,150,000
Yi	5,453,564	Xibe	83,683	Miao	7,660,000
Miao	5,021,175	Salar	69,135	Hui	7,600,000
Manchu	4,304,981	Bulang	58,473	Uygur	6,610,000
Tibetan	3,874,875	Gelo	54,164	Yi	6,610,000
Mongolian	3,411,367	Maonan	38,159	Mongolian	5,200,000
Tujia	2,836,814	Tajik	26,600	Tibetan	4,740,000
Bouyei	2,119,345	Pumi	24,238	Tujia	4,400,000
Korean	1,765,204	Nu	22,896	Dong	2,390,000
Dong	1,426,400	Achang	20,433	Yao	2,110,000
Yao	1,411,967	Ewenki	19,398	Bouyei	1,650,000
Bai	1,132,224	Uzbek	12,213	Korean	1,310,000
Hani	1,058,806	Deang	12,297	Bai	1,190,000
Kazak	907,546	Jing	13,108	Hani	1,070,000
Dai	839,496	Jinuo	11,962	Other	8,080,000
Li	887,107	Yugur	10,568		
Lisu	481,884	Bonan	9,017		
She	371,965	Drung	4,633		
Lahu	304,256	Tatar	4,122		
Va	298,611	Oroqen	4,103		
Shui	286,908	Russian	2,917		
Dongxiang	279,523	Gaoshan**	1,650		
Naxi	251,592	Hezhen	1,489		
Tu	159,632	Moinba	1,140		
Kirgiz	113,386	Lhoba	1,066		
Qiang	102,815	Other (nationality not yet de-termined)	799,705		

Source: *Zhongguo tongji nianjian* (Chinese Statistical Yearbook) (1986), pp. 97f; *Far Eastern Economic Review* (Aug. 25, 1988), 30.
*January 1988.
**Excluding Taiwan.

sion, nationality cadres, nationality territories, etc. The Chinese draw no distinction between people (*minzu*), nation (*minzu*), nationality (*minzu*), and ethnos (*minzu*). This of course causes problems in defining terms.

Although there is no exact Chinese definition of the term "national minority," from the Chinese perspective it would imply an ethnic group that is relatively small numerically compared with the largest nationality, and that is distinguished from society at large and from the Han by certain specifically national characteristics. For example, the Hui in China are actually less an ethnic than a religious minority (Moslems), but they have been recognized as an ethnic minority on the basis of common characteristics and a separate development (see the Chinese concept of nation in Chapter 3), which demonstrates that purely ethnic factors need not always be decisive. Ethnic factors are also present alongside religious factors, and religion is undoubtedly a part of the culture of this nationality (although this is officially disputed in China).

The acknowledgment of the existence of national minorities and of different nationalities means that the existence of a national question and a nationality problem has been acknowledged as well. In a similar vein, the question of special treatment for these minorities in a unified state comes up. And a nuance to the term national minority implies something more in the Chinese context, namely, preclusion of the right of secession from the state polity.

The terms national minority and nationality are largely identical in China (see Chapter 3). *Minzu* is used to refer to all of China's nationalities, the Han as well as the minorities. In common usage the term, on the one hand, indicates legal equality and, on the other, documents that all of China's nationalities are subordinate to a higher authority (the state).

The term nationality as it is commonly used in the West, with its roots in international law, may within reason be applied to China as well: nationalities are to a greater or lesser degree subject to a higher authority (in contrast to the nation, which has the sovereign right to determine its political destiny). At most, they possess rights of self-administration of their territory, which, however, is a part of the larger state. A state that grants the right to territorial autonomy and to participation in the exercise of state power to the peoples and nationalities under its dominion is a "nationality-state" (in contrast to a national state, in which the nation in control of the state exercises exclusive dominion). In a nationality-state all nationalities are formally equal and do not question the integrity of the state. This term

Table 1.2

Chinese Language Groups

Language Group	Minorities
Han	Hui, She
Sino-Tibetan	
Sino-Thai	Zhuang, Bouyei, Dai, Li, Mulam, Shui, Dong, Maonan, Gelo
Tibeto-Burmese	Tibetan, Jingpo, Drung, Qiang, Yi, Hani, Lisu, Nu, Bai, Naxi, Jinuo, Lahu, Tujia, Achang, Moinba, Lhoba, Pumi
Miao-Yao	Miao, Yao
Altaic	
Turkish	Uygur, Kazak, Kirgiz, Uzbek, Tatar, Salar, Yugur
Mongolian	Mongolian, Daur, Dongxiang, Tu, Bonan, Yugur
Tungusic	Manchu, Xibe, Hezhen, Oroqen, Ewenki
Korean	Korean
Austric	
Austro-Asiatic	Va, Bulang, Deang
Austronesian	Gaoshan (Taiwan)
Indo-European	
Iranian	Tajik
Slavic	Russian

differs in content from the term multinational state, which merely implies that there are several peoples within one state polity.

The nationalities of China

There are presently fifty-six recognized nationalities in China (see Table 1.1), of which the Han Chinese are numerically the largest with 937 million (1982). The fifty-five "national minorities" (*shaoshu minzu*), which according to the population census of 1982 totaled 67 million persons (6.7 percent of the total population), constitute a group of considerable size.[28] The largest minority, the Zhuang in South China, comprised in that year 14 million persons. The smallest

Figure 1.1. **Sample Scripts of Chinese National Minorities.**

The Yi from the Lingshan mountains

Mongolian

Ancient Naxi hieroglyphs

˩˧., ˩˩₁ FI. M WO, GU., NY-·
A₁ B₁ HO₁ LE M. DU M-·
A M TI.. LE BV., DU., M-·
˩I., NI₁ M˥₁ XO₁ N₁ JI., ∧--·
˩I., NI₁ V., dU., N₁ ZO₁ ∧=
L.. TI., TI., ४₁ X∩. MO., SI.-·
L∀₁ LO., LO., ४₁ LU. MO., SI.--
X∩. MO., Z., B˥₁ B˥₁ O JO₁-·
LU. MO., Z., JU₁ BI., O JO, =
NY, WV₁ M ४₁ M˥₁, L., ˩V₁--
XO., MV, L∀₁ JU D∃₁ L., O-·
LO., XU₁ Y₁ WE. M˥., L., NY--
N. Z₁ NY, ४₁ JU₁ L., O--
X., MI DE KW CO.. NYI., NY--
N. MI., DE., KW ˩O₁ NYI., NY-·
X.. MI DE KW MO₁ JO, B˥-·
N. MI., DE KW X∩. JO, B˥.,=
L₁ NYI A₁ B₁ TV. BV G˥,-·
T˥, NYI A., M.. TV. M. G˥₁-·
MO₁ RO.. L., O BV.. G˥₁ ˩V₁-·
X∩. N∃₁ L., O M. G˥₁ ˩V₁-·
A₁ B₁ MO₁ LE BV., DU., M-·
A M TI., LE WO, DU., M-·
X.. MI MO₁ FI. ɔI., O JO₁-·

The Lahu

ᥓᥴᥖᥳᥑ ᥖᥭᥴ ᥝᥨᥰᥑᥲᥛᥴ ᥖᥱᥩ �

ᥑᥨᥖᥲ�294ᥴ ᥖᥐᥙᥴᥲ246 ᥙᥭᥴ ᥝᥨᥡᥳ4ᥖᥭ, ᥝᥨᥱᥝᥨᥱ4ᥧᥰᥝᥨᥱᥲᥝᥨᥱᥴᥭᥰ ᥝᥨᥱᥳᥝᥨᥰᥑᥴ. ᥝᥩᥱᥳᥙᥴᥩᥰᥝᥴᥩ4ᥖᥖᥭᥥ4ᥴ ᥝᥙᥱᥥ4ᥛᥥᥩᥰᥩᥡᥰᥙᥴᥴᥦ ᥩᥡᥱᥩᥥᥩ, ᥝᥩᥴ ᥖᥩᥝᥰ4ᥝᥖ ᥐᥝᥩᥡᥴᥩᥥᥝᥬᥰᥖᥛᥰᥖᥩᥴᥙᥨᥰᥖᥩᥝᥰ4ᥑ.

ᥖᥭᥴᥲ294ᥰᥝᥥᥩ4ᥛᥖᥝᥬᥦᥝᥫᥝᥛᥝᥬᥦᥡᥥᥝ᥮4ᥩᥡᥴ, ᥖᥭᥲᥱᥛᥳᥒᥫᥫᥖᥭᥦᥡ4ᥩᥥ4ᥩᥝᥬ ᥝᥩᥝᥨᥰᥴᥖᥝᥩᥛᥦᥒᥡᥩᥴᥖᥥ4ᥩᥰᥲ, ᥙᥩᥴᥴᥖᥝᥩᥝᥨᥰᥴ4ᥙᥖᥰᥝᥥᥙᥛᥲᥛᥖ4ᥙᥖᥲᥥ4ᥝᥩᥡᥩ4ᥩᥦ4ᥩ. ᥙᥰᥲᥲᥝᥝᥩ ᥩᥡᥩᥰᥲᥝᥰᥦ, ᥖᥝ4ᥲᥰᥛᥴᥝᥖᥨᥝᥩᥰ4ᥴᥙᥩᥡ4ᥰᥴ, ᥙᥡᥳᥴᥛᥰᥨᥩᥖᥝ4ᥩᥲᥲᥝᥝ4ᥲᥰᥲᥝᥥᥨᥰᥴᥝᥩ4ᥩᥲᥖᥰᥝᥝᥨᥩ4ᥴᥝᥴᥩ.

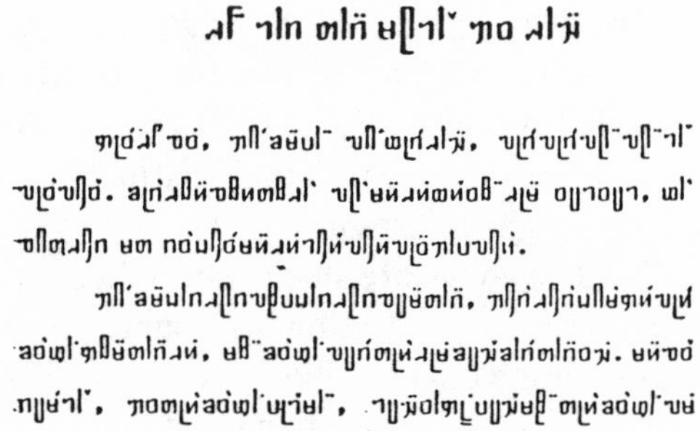

The Dai from Dehong

MA PRI LAIKA KA NGA AI

MA PRI GO LAIKA KA NGA AI.

MA KAI HTE MA NO BAI SA WA

MARA AI.

LAIKA KA MA NNA BRA WA

MASAI.

The Jingpo

group, the hunter tribe of Luoba in Tibet, numbers a little more than 1,000. According to a random sample census from 1987, the ethnic minorities accounted for 8 percent (about 80 million people) of the total population.[29]

Many Chinese nationalities have kin beyond China's borders. Miao, Hani, Dai, Jing, Jingpo, Lahu, Lisu, Va, Yao, Yi, and Zhuang also exist in Vietnam, Laos, Thailand, and Burma; most Koreans live in Korea; a large number of Mongols live in the Mongolian People's Republic; Kazak, Kirgiz, Tajik, Tatar, Mongolian, Uygur, Daur, Ewenki, Oroqen, Hezhen, and others also live in the Soviet Union. The migration of minorities to other countries during times of political repression in China and the influx of the same minorities from other countries, such as Vietnam, Laos, or Burma, in times of political crisis, points out how China's nationality policy and the policies of its neighbors are intertwined.

The data above are sufficient to illustrate the potential explosiveness of the nationality question in a country such as China. But one must also know that the ethnic minorities inhabit 50–60 percent of Chinese territory, principally the outlying and border regions, which are as important for their rich deposits of raw materials as they are for defense. The country's internal stability and its defense capacity are to a large degree dependent on the behavior of minorities. In case of war, for example, the attitude adopted by China's minorities could rapidly tip the balance in the adversary's favor. If such an adversary (e.g., the Soviet Union), were able to win over the minorities in Xinjiang, Tibet, and Inner Mongolia, large areas of the country could be torn away without problem, transformed into vassal states, or annexed by the Soviet Union for the purpose of ''reunification of the nationalities.''[30]

A perusal of the list of language groups in Table 1.2 provides a further picture of the diversity of China's nationalities. Only two groups, the Hui and the She, use the Han Chinese language and form of writing. The Yugur have two different languages; other groups such as the Jing so far have been classified in no language group. Manchu has been tending toward extinction since the end of the last imperial dynasty (1911).

When the People's Republic was founded in 1949, eleven written languages of ethnic minorities were in regular use, and seven others were used sporadically. Since then, twenty-five written languages for ethnic minorities have been codified through the creation of new scripts, some based on the Latin language.[31] Figure 1.1 shows the variety of ethnic sources evident in the scripts of six minorities.

The diversity of the groups and languages is matched by an equally diverse spectrum of social relations. Some of the nationalities maintained slaves and slave markets, serfs, and head-hunting into the 1950s. Some of the small groups lived as hunters and gatherers in remote primeval forests or mountain territories, and in some of these class structures had not yet formed.

In the sixties and seventies, very little was heard outside of China about the ethnic minorities and their actual situation. They were, of course, present in China's foreign propaganda, but then only as beaming happy figures clad in bright and many-colored garments, acclaiming the current popular political line. Today we know that the reality was somewhat different. Since the end of the fifties and especially during the Cultural Revolution (1966–1976), there were strong attempts through massive pressure and occasionally force to bring the ethnic minorities to heel and to assimilate them. They were divested of all special rights, their languages and modes of writing were forbidden, and their manners and customs suppressed. Although all Chinese (including the Han) suffered during the Cultural Revolution, the minorities experienced the particular indignity of being coerced to renounce most of their national identities. Tibet, where almost all the convents and religious edifices were destroyed, is one of the saddest examples of the nationality policy of that time. Economic and cultural backwardness, alienation between the Han Chinese and the minorities, and, especially for the smaller groups, a growing loss of national and cultural identities were the consequences.

The "barbarians"

Throughout the history, the territory which today is China has hosted a multitude of peoples.[32] Chinese history is at the same time a history of vast migratory movements and of decline, genesis, and fusion of diverse peoples. The Han Chinese themselves were the product of the intermixing of many tribes on the territory of what is now China. But the Han, who were tillers of the soil, were even in those early times contemptuous of the peoples around them, the hunters and gatherers or nomads. For the Han, distinguishing among these peoples amounted solely to the differences in where beyond the horizon they lived, their distance from the center of the world (i.e., where the emperor had his seat), and the degree of their subjugation. The peoples were simply classified as the Di (north), the Yi (east), the Rong (west), and the Man barbarians (south).[33]

But over the centuries, the non-Han peoples who inhabited central China in ancient times were nevertheless pushed progressively into the borderlands by the Han. Confucianism, the ideology of the state throughout all the Chinese dynasties, despised these so-called "barbarians," but called for a policy of nonviolent assimilation through the imposition of Han-Chinese values rather than through a policy of extermination. These Confucian ideas run consistently throughout the history of nationality relations in China.

The Han Chinese considered their culture and civilization to be the center of the world. The neighboring "barbarian" tribes were forced to send regular tributes to the Chinese emperor. In return the chieftains of the tribes received official positions and seals, but at a lower status than the Han. The barbarians' acceptance of these signified their subjugation to the Chinese court. The court's policy was not to conquer and occupy them, but rather to have them administer themselves; in turn, the court had the responsibility of dealing with the areas' social problems and helping them militarily in case of an attack.

The various peoples on Chinese territory wove intricate networks of interconnection and influence over the course of history. Contacts were not only belligerent; there was also lively trade and mutual enrichment. Indeed, some of the imperial dynasties were ruled by non-Han peoples who had over time been unable to withstand the extremely powerful cultural influence of the Han culture and in the end had became sinified.

The Republic of China, formed after the fall of the last dynasty in 1911, only partially acknowledged the existence of ethnic minorities in China. Its founder, Sun Yat-sen, included Mongolians, Manchu, Tibetans, and Moslems among the Chinese people.[34] However, he called for gradual assimilation of the minorities in the nation's interest. Although Sun Yat-sen reconsidered his ideas shortly before his death,[35] his successor, Chiang Kai-shek, denied the existence of different nationalities. For him, the non-Han peoples were only "branch clans" of the Han, who were to be deliberately assimilated.[36]

Nationality relations
from a historical perspective

Historically seen, China could be said to have been a multinational state for thousands of years, but it has by no means always constituted a unified state structure. Although a sequence of non-Han peoples did at different times over the course of China's history subjugate the ethnic majority, the Han, and found their own dynasties (e.g., the Liao, Jin, Yuan, and Qing dynasties), nonetheless it was primarily the Han who subjugated the other peoples and exacted tributes from them.

Although the non-Han brought elements of their own cultures to China and made considerable contributions to its development, it has only been in the last few years that this truth has again found an audience in China.[37]

The history of the peoples of the "middle kingdom" was by no means exclusively a history of internal wars. There are quite enough examples of peaceful coexistence, cultural enrichment, and even common struggles engaged in jointly by Han and non-Han. Such instances include the Taiping rebellion (1850–1864), in which equality was demanded for all peoples of China and which was supported by the non-Han peoples in southern and southwest China;[38] the role of the non-Han in the revolution of 1911, which led to the fall of the Qing dynasty;[39] and the participation of the national minorities in the clashes with the encroaching imperialist powers in the nineteenth and twentieth centuries.[40]

An important question once again being debated in China is whether the national minorities in today's China have always been "Chinese people," or whether they have constituted independent states in the course of China's history. This question was at one time taboo; for example, anyone who wrote on the struggles of the non-Han peoples for independence from the Han was accused of "local nationalism" during the campaign of "Anti-Rightist Struggle" in 1957–58.[41] If the history of a national minority was studied, it was always from the standpoint of its allegiance to China, with the principal trend being that of good relations with the Han. Efforts of minorities to achieve independence, or even the concept of independence itself, were passed over in silence or at best attributed to a few "reactionaries" who wished to "undermine national unity." But the fact is that independent political states of non-Han people did exist on the territory of what is today China, although they were all short-lived. For example, the Nanzhao Empire of the Yi, Bai, and Dai in southwest China, which existed from 730 A.D. into the thirteenth century, was effectively independent in the eighth century (although only due to a misguided policy of the Tang court and against the Nanzhao's will). At the end of the eighth century, the Nanzhao Empire resubmitted itself to the sovereignty of the Tang dynasty.[42]

The controversy over this is demonstrated by an article in the periodical *Sixiang zhanxian*, which contests this independence with the curt reference to the "blood ties of all nationalities of our countries,"[43] and minimizes the disputes over the *de facto* independence of non-Han people during the course of history on the territory of today's China. However, an article by Li Gui in the periodical of the Central South Nationalities Institute in Wuhan once again ventured the view that there have been repeated instances of independence of non-Han people over the course of Chinese history. In contrast to other scholars who say that such independence has existed, but that it had been detrimental to the development of China as a whole, Li Gui avers that this independence enriched China.[44] Accordingly, it is now being conceded that national minorities have made major contributions to the country's development.[45]

The official, rigid historical picture is burdened by the necessity of having to demonstrate that the ethnic minorities were always a part of the "Chinese family of nationalities." Were it acknowledged that non-Han peoples did enjoy a *de facto* independence over the course of Chinese history, it would certainly help to dissipate this narrow picture and to replace it with a realistic depiction of history that is closer to the truth. A hidden factor in this obsessive search for a proof of independence, however, is the fear that some nationalities might raise the cry for secession on historical grounds.

The historical relations among China's nationalities have once again become a subject of scholarly discussion. Wars of non-Han people against the Han have long been portrayed as "aggression" or "destruction" in Chinese history books, while Han campaigns of conquest against these people have been depicted as "useful for the unity of the country," "in the interest of progress and development of the national minorities," or "in the interest of historical development." All wars of non-Han peoples against the Han have been dubbed "reactionary," and the converse case as "progressive." Purportedly, the Han disseminated their more developed social structure to the regions of other nationalities through their wars. Conversely, the other nationalities attempted to "impose backward economic and social relations" on the Han. A similar double standard was for a long time applied to historical personalities of ethnic minorities: those whose actions served the unity of the country were progressive, but all others were reactionary.[46] In essence, everything was subordinated to the Han version of history, making an objective assessment of the actual process impossible. The question of who oppressed or threatened whom, and what interests were behind a war, or what were the causes of conflicts and assorted frictions among the different peoples, were not dealt with.

In 1981, a scholarly conference was held on this very topic, and chauvinist positions of the past were criticized. But there is still no unified stand on the question of the historical relations among China's nationalities. At present, unanimity exists only on the point that, in assessing wars among China's different nationalities and in evaluating national heroes, a new set of standards must be used.

An article in the periodical of the Central Institute for Nationalities in Beijing said that all peoples who have at any time lived on the territory of what is today China—even if the group no longer exists—are Chinese, for "if one said that they are not Chinese, then to what country should they then belong?"[47] By this reasoning, even peoples who temporarily established a political power of their own would belong to China, would be Chinese and not foreigners. All these people contributed, it is stated, to China's development. The article, while conceding that there is still no unified view on this question, does seem to propose a reclassification of the ethnic minorities living in China today not as "aliens" but rather as members of the Chinese people. The article is accordingly subtitled: "Keep to the principle of equality of national minorities in historical research." This line of thought not only provides the rationale for how and why Tibet is a part of the Chinese state polity, but also how and why it is legitimate for China to lay claim to regions and nationalities that today ("temporarily") are no longer a part of the Chinese polity (e.g., Outer Mongolia, Korea). Although this formulation is more than questionable, it does reveal the underpinnings of the Chinese concept of nation.[48]

The European concept of nation defines "nation" as the sum of the government plus its people, whereas the Chinese defines nation as a historically legitimated territory plus the whole population on this territory. The European definition is political-subjective, the Chinese historical-objective. Similar differences are found in the definition of nationality. In Europe it means nationality=citizenship (an etatistic concept); in China nationality=one is member of an ethnic group that historically is part of the Chinese nation (an historical-ethnical concept). Only by understanding this difference between the European and the Chinese concepts can we understand the Chinese evaluation of questions like Tibet.

2
The Cultural Revolution and the Ethnic Minorities

The Cultural Revolution (1966–1976) followed the same lines in the regions of the national minorities as it did in the Han regions.[1] There was, however, a distinct, additional element of renewed suppression of nationality identity throughout this time that targeted the minorities in particular.

The impetus behind the Cultural Revolution came from the group around Mao Zedong who wanted to assert their "line" and eliminate their enemies once and for all. The opening shot was Mao's statement that a large number of "representatives of the bourgeoisie" and "counterrevolutionary revisionists" had already "crept" into the party, the government, and the army, as well as into all areas of the cultural sector. Those holding power in the party who were "taking the road of capitalism" had banded together into a "bourgeois headquarters" in the Chinese Communist Party (CCP) Central Committee, which was pursuing a "revisionist line" and had representatives in all areas. The struggles of the past had not led to a resolution of this problem, and only a cultural revolution, a political revolution, with broad mobilization of the masses, could reinstate the "proletarian line."[2]

The above cannonade shows that this was indeed a "battle of the lines." All opponents of Mao's line were summarily relegated to the classification of persons in power taking the capitalist road. This facilitated their removal as well as allowed Mao's line to prevail.[3]

Today the party admits that the Cultural Revolution inflicted "the most grievous reverses and losses on the party, the country, and the people since the founding of the People's Republic." Mao's chief arguments had corresponded neither to Marxism-Leninism nor to the Chinese reality, but were based on a false assessment of the class situation in China and the political situation in the party and the state. This led to "no social progress of any kind," with "disastrous consequences" for all of China's nationalities.[4]

Relying on the theory that even in socialism the national issue was ultimately a "class issue," the "ultraleft forces" in China (represented by the "Gang of Four") evidently hoped to do away with the national issue by forcing "class struggle." The earlier nationality policy, which had been based in part on recognition of the particularities and differences of the national minorities and their regions, was labeled a "bourgeois reactionary line." The policy of the United Front was called "capitulationism," and the former president of the state Liu Shaoqi was criticized because he had written ("On Nationalism and Internationalism," 1948) that "national problems are *linked* to class problems"[5] (author's emphasis), which was seen as denying that the national issue was a class issue. His earlier demands for regional autonomy of the ethnic minorities were interpreted as "opposition to national unity and advocation of national separatism,"[6] and his accession to the 1954 constitutional clause on regional autonomy as "obliterating the essence of the dictatorship of the proletariat."[7] His appeal for prudence and circumspection in the redistribution of the land and the reform of customs and manners was now seen as "suppression of the revolutionary demands of the national minorities for liberation" and his appeal for peaceful reform as "obliteration of the class struggle."[8]

A draft of the party constitution circulated in Shanghai on behalf of the "masses of Shanghai" in 1968 stated:

> The old party constitution stresses only the special characteristics of the nationalities and the conducting of social reforms, according to their own wishes, but not the party's leadership and the socialist revolution. It says, "the development of many national minorities has been restricted" and "the party must make a special effort to improve the position of the various national minorities." By emphasizing nationalism to the exclusion of patriotism and internationalism, it in reality creates national schisms. The broad revolutionary masses maintain that the following directive from

Chairman Mao should be stressed in the new party constitution of the Ninth Congress: "National struggle is, in the final analysis, a question of class struggle." The unity of all nationalities on the basis of the thought of Chairman Mao Zedong and on the socialist road should be stressed.[9]

The concept that minorities and their territories were distinctive was again rejected, and all agencies for the minorities (nationality commissions, institutes, schools, etc.) were disbanded. All special privileges for members of national minorities were eliminated: henceforth, they were to be treated the same as the Han. This was justified by claiming that special treatment would keep the minorities from being assimilated into Chinese society and would prevent them from participating in the revolution on an equal footing.

This view was expressed, for example, in the party constitutions that were adopted at the Ninth (1969), Tenth (1973), and Eleventh (1977) Congresses of the CCP. The paragraph of the 1956 constitution which dealt with the minorities[10] was expunged.[11] The minorities were no longer even mentioned except peripherally (as in the constitution of the Eleventh Party Congress).

Nationality policy

The Cultural Revolution made extensive revisions in the policies concerning national minorities.

1. It was denied (mainly by the "ultraleft" forces) that China was a multinational country, and declared that the nationality issue was settled and that the nationality policy was no longer needed.[12]

2. The minorities and their territories were no longer to be labeled "special" or "backward,"[13] and no special economic policy was to be pursued for these regions. (A main charge against Liu Shaoqi, condemned in the Cultural Revolution, was that he had spoken of the "special features of the minority regions" and their "backwardness," and had demanded special treatment to deal with the specific conditions in these regions.[14]) Traditional products for the minorities were no longer produced or grown,[15] and cultural traditions were denied through such pronouncements as: "They should live in houses instead of tents, wear normal clothes instead of their costumes, pigtails

instead of turbans, and they should eat and drink in messhalls."[16]

3. The policy of national regional autonomy was condemned as creating "independent regions" and "dividing the nation," and the autonomous units were dissolved in many places (such as the Xishuangbanna Autonomous Prefecture of the Dai).[17] Autonomy ceased to exist,[18] and even special financial allowances by the central government were stopped.[19]

4. Natural resources of the minority regions were destroyed by a mistaken economic policy that ordered, for example, that certain types of rice be planted regardless of the area's special agricultural conditions. Arable land and pasture were destroyed and forests chopped down, upsetting the ecological balance in many regions and causing desertification, the drying up of water sources, and soil erosion.[20] In areas that had traditionally raised livestock, the minorities were forced to destroy their pastures, plant grain, and become farmers, which led to a drastic decrease in livestock (see chapter 6). Outside sources of income of the peasants (secondary occupations of families, private plots of land, private livestock, free markets) were restricted or abolished. Intense poverty overtook many minority territories, and some of them even fell below the level of 1949.[21]

5. Languages and scripts, customs and manners, were condemned as backward, and an attempt was made to abolish them officially.[22] The manners and customs were termed the "Four Old Things" (si jiu: old thinking, old culture, old morality, and old customs) and as such were a prime target of the "smashing."[23] Traditional holidays of the minorities were forbidden, and those who celebrated them were often arrested as "counterrevolutionaries."[24] Minorities were not allowed to wear their national costumes in some places, and selling specialty goods for minorities was outlawed. Factories that made minority products were shut down, and skilled craftsmen were labeled "bourgeois authorities."[25] In many places minorities were forced to abandon their religious traditions (see chapter 7).

Of the written scripts, only five were allowed (Mongolian, Tibetan, Uygur, Kazak, and Korean), but even their use was restricted.[26] Only Chinese was to be spoken at meetings,[27] and in many places it was a "misdemeanor" to use one's native language.[28] The presses of nationality publications were also closed, and newspapers and radio broadcasts in minority languages ceased.

6. Almost all schools and colleges for minorities were disbanded. The nationalities institutes were viewed as "hothouses for budding revisionists," and it was determined that their "historical mission" had been accomplished.[29] In many minority regions only Han—and no local language—was the language of instruction in the schools. The number of individuals belonging to minorities who could attend college dropped, and the illiteracy rate increased.[30]

7. Minority cadres were designated "culturally inferior" and "sinister pullers of the strings of the tribal chieftains." They were said to lack proficiency, to have difficulty organizing activities, etc. Many times, minority cadres were replaced by Han cadres, and their training and advanced education were discontinued.[31]

8. The health practices of the minorities were strictly curtailed as "superstitious." Their traditional medicine, very advanced in some respects, was called "unscientific, feudal, and backward." Thus, there was a lack of traditional physicians and medics, the principal health providers in these regions.[32]

9. Minority songs, dance, films, folk songs, operas, and the like were called "feudal, capitalist, revisionist, poisonous weeds." For the most part, they were prohibited or "experimentally cleansed," that is, adapted to Han taste.[33] The traditional song fests of the minorities in southwest China were also prohibited.[34] As for literature, no minority writer dared write anything during the Cultural Revolution; most writers were persecuted and their writings banned.[35]

The list of prohibitions and indignities goes on and on. In conversations and visits to the scene, or in discussions with members of national minorities, the lingering effects remain evident. For example, in Inner Mongolia, it was said that the Cultural Revolution had claimed more lives among the Mongols than the massacres of the famed "Slayer of Mongols" (a famous Han general) of the Ming dynasty. According to the indictment against the Gang of Four, 346,000 persons in the Autonomous Region of Inner Mongolia were wrongfully accused and persecuted under the pretext of having formed a so-called "Revolutionary People's Party of Inner Mongolia"; these persecutions claimed 16,222 lives.[36] Because this fictitious party was theoretically pursuing separatist goals, allegedly led by the Mongol Ulanhu (since then rehabilitated, deceased in 1988), and because the "unity between the nationalities had been undermined" by this affair,[37] those persecuted must have been almost exclusively Mongols. If the Mongolian component of the population of Inner Mongolia was 1.45 million in 1965, then more than 20 percent of the Mongolian population there was persecuted in connection with this affair, and more than 1 percent killed. In addition, the area of the Autonomous Region of Inner Mongolia was reduced by nearly half in 1969 and 1970 (the official reason being that it was necessary as a security measure vis-à-vis the Soviet Union); the region was not restored to its original form until 1979.

An exhibit of clothing and ornaments of the Li nationality in Beijing (1980) displayed chests of fabric shreds and shattered ornaments that had been destroyed during the Cultural Revolution by the Red Guards. In Jinghong, the capital city of the Xishuangbanna Autonomous Prefecture of the Dai, in 1978 not a single book in the Dai script could be found in the bookshops, nor was the Dai language or script taught at the teacher training college of Jinghong. Furthermore, the library of the college had neither books nor periodicals in Dai.

The outcome of the Cultural Revolution

Today, it is actually admitted by the CCP that a "fascist dictatorship was exercised over the national minorities," a "feudal, fascist, reactionary nationality policy" had been carried out, and a policy of "forced assimilation" had been pursued.[38] As early as 1980 the newspaper *Minzu tuanjie* wrote that the principle of equality of the nationalities was not being observed, and that the minorities had suffered insults and considerable discrimination in jobs and education. Their dress and holidays had been sharply supervised and restricted, the education and promotion of minority workers were reined in, state funds for the economy and culture of the minority regions were simply used for other purposes by the executive agencies, the scripts and languages were outlawed and no longer used, and no attention was given to the development of the respective regions or their economy in the exploitation of raw materials. Pastures, forests, and mineral deposits were in many cases ruined. The higher authorities cared little about the living conditions, production, culture, education, or health of these regions.[39]

Little wonder that faith in the CCP has been shaken,[40] or that the relations among the nationalities are "tense."[41]

The constitution of 1975 curtailed all rights of the nationalities and in their place made class struggle its objective. Stricken from the constitution were the prohibition of prejudice and discrimination against members of ethnic minorities; the freedom to preserve or reform languages and scripts, manners and customs; the right of regional autonomy; the specific pronouncements on the right of self government and the agencies of self government. It was proclaimed:

> The higher state organs must guarantee the autonomous organs of all regions with national autonomy the full exercise of this autonomy and should actively support all national minorities in the socialist revolution and the construction of socialism.[42]

This bland statement left the nature of autonomy completely open and allowed arbitrary interpretation. Not only was support to be rendered to the minorities in the "socialist revolution" and in the "construction of socialism," but also any demand which the higher authorities thought contradicted this end (such as tailoring the development of the economy to the minority region characteristics, preservation of manners and customs, etc.) could be rejected on the basis of this clause. At the same time, the right of a defendant to use the language and script of his nationality in court was repealed; from now on, cases could only be heard in the Han language and the Han script, whether or not the defendant could understand the proceedings.

Humiliation, insults, oppression, and an attempt at forced assimilation; destruction of the ecological equilibrium and ruinous exploitation; economic plundering of the minority regions: these were the consequences of the Cultural Revolution for the national minorities and their regions. It is no wonder that relations between the Han and minorities remain embittered in many places; it will take much time to heal these wounds.

3

Nationality and Ethnic Identification: Recognition as a Minority

The 1982 population census showed that the nationality identity of 800,000 persons (1.2 percent of all minority members) had not yet been definitively classified.[1] Although this figure seems relatively small, it does bring up the question of how the term "nationality" is actually defined in China and why, after four decades of the People's Republic, 800,000 persons still have no official nationality.

The Chinese concept of "nationality"

As noted in chapter 1, the Chinese language has never distinguished among peoples, nation, nationality, and ethnos. All these entities are lumped together under the single term "minzu." This causes definition problems, especially since many different peoples, ethnic groups, tribes, etc., in various stages of development and periods of history all fall under this term. It is only since the early 1980s that Chinese social scientists have been laboring to give this term a more precise definition.[2]

Since the fifties, Chinese scholars have routinely referred to the definition of nationality given in the Marxist-Leninist literature, which Stalin first formulated in 1914 in his monograph *Marxism and the National Question*:

> A nation is a historically formed stable community of people arising on the basis of common language, common territory, common economic life, and a typical cast of mind manifested in a common culture.[3]

In the early sixties, there was a debate taking place in the USSR on this Stalinist concept of nation, as this concept neither corresponded to present realities in the developing countries nor helped to redefine nationality relations in the Soviet Union.[4] But this discussion was curtailed in 1968 under pressure from the party leadership. The periodical *Voprosy istorii* summed up the results in 1970 by noting that ". . . the definition of nation formulated by J. W. Stalin sums up everything that Marx, Engels, and Lenin have said on the question of its essence and principal characteristics."[5]

But Stalin's definition is not as dogmatically applied in China as it is in the Soviet Union. A debate in China on Stalin's definition has been unfolding in the wake of China's liberalization after 1979. Very few scholars have taken the position that Stalin's definition was "definitive and undisputable" for "all" nationalities.[6] Instead, the majority of Chinese experts agree that Stalin's definition had its origins in European conditions and referred specifically to capitalist societies. But different opinions arise as to whether it might nonetheless serve as a guideline for determining nationality in China.[7]

Chinese conditions do not easily incorporate the Stalinist concept. Among the reasons for this are:

1. *Lack of common language.* In China there are minorities who speak Chinese—for example, the Manchus, who headed the last imperial dynasty from 1644 to 1911, and who became largely sinicized during the course of their rule over China; and the Hui, a Chinese-speaking Islamic minority. In the case of other minorities, one segment of a minority may speak differently from another—some of the Yugur, who are probably descendants of the Huns, speak a Turkish language, while the others speak a Mongolian one;[8] the Jingpo also speak a variety of languages, some of which are totally unlike the others.[9]

2. *Lack of common territory.* For historical reasons, some segments of minorities live in different regions, in some cases quite far from one another. For example, the Hui are scattered over the entire country; there are Manchus in many cities in north and central China; the Mongols inhabit the north, northwest, east, and southwest of China. Often several nationalities live in the same village, township, or county ("mixed territories"). In these cases, there is no common territory of only one nationality.

3. *Lack of a common economic life.* In regions where nationalities

have lived in close proximity for centuries, a unified economic life has evolved for several nationalities, with common marketplaces and economic centers.

4. *Lack of a common culture.* The influence of the major nationalities on the minor ones is considerable in mixed territories. In addition, the Han culture for centuries has exerted its influence on many minorities who by now in many cases are partly sinicized.

The application of Stalin's criteria to ethnic minorities in China therefore seems absurd, especially in view of his affirmation that if just one of these characteristics is lacking, there can be no talk of a nation.

Then why do Chinese scholars continue to refer to Stalin? Common language, common territory, and common culture are decisive criteria, but they are not sufficient, as a glance at Chinese conditions will show. Thus Stalin's criteria are employed "flexibly" (i.e., adapted to Chinese conditions) along with another characteristic, namely "self-consciousness"—the idea that an ethnic group see itself as an independent nationality.[10]

> For ethnic identification we use Marxist categories. But we do not only proceed from history, economics, habits and customs, language, cast of mind, and historical development, we also of course respect the national will of the nationality concerned. On the other hand, a people cannot be categorized as an independent nationality if the national will is at variance with scientific knowledge.[11]

Beyond that, it is said that two principal factors must be taken into account in classification: the scientific basis, and the will of the community.[12]

Interestingly, the Chinese apply a criterion that the Austrian Social Democrat Otto Bauer put forth in 1924, but that Stalin vehemently rejected: national consciousness. Bauer defined this consciousness as follows:

> Seen in isolation, national consciousness is nothing more than the knowledge that I have certain characteristic features, physical properties, certain cultural goods, specific aspirations, in common with my ethnic comrades, and that in this respect I differ from those people who belong to other nations, and this gives theoretical depth to the knowledge that I am a part of the same history as they.[13]

The debate over the definition of nation and Stalin's criteria continues. An article in the periodical *Guizhou minzu yanjiu* proposed that, for the purpose of determining nationality in China, two or three of Stalin's criteria could easily be omitted. But the "specific cast of mind," which would include the concept of the people's own will and national self-conception, should not be one of those omitted. This applies particularly to such nationalities as the Manchu or the Hui who use both the Han language and writing, did not inhabit a common territory, and had no common economic life, but who nevertheless are recognized as independent nationalities.[14]

An article in *Yunnan shehui kexue* proposes the following modifications to Stalin's definition:

> A nation is a historically evolved stable community of human beings, born on the basis of common language, common territory, common economic life, and common national consciousness, and national sentiment.[15]

Whereas Stalin's definition applied only to "modern peoples," the latter one is universal. This definition, however, not only omits the criterion of common culture but also is unable to explain why the Manchu and Hui are independent nationalities.

The Chinese discussion on the concept of nation shows that while, on the one hand, the Stalinist definition still has a hold, on the other hand, it is difficult to apply to Chinese circumstances. As in the Soviet Union, Chinese scholars are confronted with the dilemma that a real universal definition has yet to be found for modern nations and nationalities.[16] But unlike in the Soviet Union, in China a consensus has been reached that scientific criteria are not sufficient for a definitive classification of an ethnic group as an independent nationality, that in addition the opinion of the members of such a group carries just as much weight.[17] Thus the Miao on Hainan Island, who from a scientific point of view are not Miao but Yao, are classified as Miao because the ethnic group insisted upon it.

The Hui are also an independent nationality although they are not different ethnically and linguistically from the Han and are dispersed throughout China. In their case, religion (Islam) is the sole common ethnic denominator. Yet Chinese scholars vehemently dispute that religion can be in any respect a criterion for nationality.

Problems of ethnic identification in the 1950s

Sun Yat-sen, the founder of the Republic of China, recognized China merely as a "republic of five nationalities" in the twenties. Later the Guomindang government simply denied the existence of ethnic minorities, regarding them rather as "branches of the Han," which made ethnic identification and classification impossible.

Since no one knew exactly how many different nationalities lived in China, in the early fifties the new government began to investigate.

Four-hundred ethnic groups responded to an initial call for registration of national minorities. However, the studies showed that a large number of those who claimed to be separate nationalities were actually members of the same group, that other different groups belonged to the same nationality but used different names, and still others were Han who for historical reasons had no clear identity of their origins.

Detailed studies and field research were initiated in 1953. By 1957, fifty-four ethnic groups were recognized as independent nationalities (the Jinuo were recognized in 1979, making fifty-five). The official recognition was granted to the nationalities by the Chinese State Council.

When they began the work of ethnic identification, the Chinese authorities and scholars were faced with the following classification problems:

—Han Chinese who had migrated into minority regions and whose descendants retained some Han language and cultural characteristics were uncertain of their nationality. They therefore registered under names that the native inhabitants had given them.

—Different Han groups migrated into the same minority region at different times. The earlier groups, long cut off from other Han, differed from the later groups in language and manners, and in some cases were discriminated against by the latter. The descendants of the earlier groups therefore demanded definition as their own ethnic minority.

—Some minorities had been torn apart over the course of history and were scattered in colonies among the Han. They had been strongly influenced by Han culture, their language had changed, they had discarded many of their national characteristics—yet they were discriminated against by the Han. Therefore they lived in their own communities, and regarded themselves as a nationality.

—Segments of a nationality had separated from the rest and migrated to other parts of the country. Although they had by and large retained the language, customs, and usages as well as historical legends of the original nationality, they had assumed new names in their new locations and registered under these names after 1949.

—Sometimes, segments of a nationality lived in different regions, formed numerous independent communities, and displayed considerable differences (as well as some similarities) with regard to both language and culture. These splintered groups nevertheless were known by the same name and regarded themselves as the same nationality.[18]

—Segments of a nationality were spread out over diverse regions and had adopted the culture and the life style of their neighboring nationality. They continued, however, to speak their original language and were known by the same name among other nationalities, and in fact considered themselves one nationality.

Case study: the Chuanqing

In identifying a nationality in China, two basic determinations had to be made: (1) whether the group was a national minority or a part of the Han nationality; and (2) if an ethnic minority, did it constitute an independent nationality or only part of such a nationality.

The case of the Chuanqing in the province of Guizhou is a good example of the complexity of the issue of nationality.

Chuanqing means "clad in black," which was the way they were distinguished from another group, the Chuanlan ("clad in blue"). (For simplicity's sake, we shall refer to them in this discussion as the "Blacks" and the "Blues.") In 1950 the Blacks, totaling about 200,000 persons, applied for recognition as a national minority, based on the following:

—their original language differed from that of the local Han population;

—the majority of them lived in their own compact communities in the countryside;

—they differed from the local Han in religious belief and in manners and customs; and

—their women wore clothing different from Han women, had different hairstyles, did not bind their feet, and were not borne on a sedan chair at their wedding, as the Han were.

The Blacks were discriminated against by the Blues, and not infrequently conflicts arose between the two. After the founding of the People's Republic, almost all the Blues registered as Han. The Blacks applied for recognition as a national minority so that they not only would receive preferential treatment from the government but also would be protected from discrimination by the Blues.

The other ethnic minorities in this region did not regard the Blacks as a minority but instead as a special group of Han, and called them the "poor Han" or "rustic Han." It seemed that the Blacks, however, did have some factors in their language, area of settlement, economic life, and behavior to certify them as a national minority.

First, scholars investigated the Blacks' language. They found that a small number of them still spoke the "old dialect," while others used the Han language with an accent peculiar to the Guizhou province. An analysis of the old dialect showed a total identity with the Han language and no affinity to the languages of other nationalities. It was determined that the Blacks spoke a dialect that had its roots in the provinces of Jiangxi, Hunan, and Hubei. They presumably spoke this dialect when they first came to Guizhou, and subsequently adopted the local dialect only in the previous fifty to sixty years.

This linguistic analysis, however, was not in itself sufficient to warrant the conclusion that the Blacks belonged to the Han nationality, since groups who speak the same language may easily belong to different nationalities. But the analysis also gave a clue to the origin of the Blacks: it indicated that they had come from neighboring provinces as documented by family genealogies, tomb inscriptions, markings on historical relics, local chronicles, and popular legend.

Thus the next step was to investigate the history of the Blacks. In 1381, the emperor who had founded the Ming dynasty sent troops to the south to destroy the remaining forces of the Yuan dynasty. On their way through the province of Guizhou, occupation troops were left behind to cultivate the land. Next came other Han who migrated from the interior, including those from the province of Jiangxi who were forced laborers in the army. These laborers settled in what is today Qingzhen, a region bordering on an area inhabited by the Yi. They and their families were called "civilian households," to distinguish them from the privileged "army households"; the army households were allotted land by the government authorities, but the civilian households had to lease land from the Yi, and so became tenant farmers. Although these immigrants had a relatively low social status, the proximity of the Han army enabled them to remain as communities separate from the Yi, and since they were economically and culturally more advanced than the Yi, they were not assimilated by the latter.

The history of the Blues was also investigated. The Blues came to Guizhou at about the same time as the Blacks. They were mostly merchants and were concentrated primarily in the cities and market centers. They had a higher political and economic status than the Blacks and were contemptuous of the Black tenant farmers.

Although the two Han groups forged an alliance in the early struggles against the Yi chieftains, the Blues gained the upper hand as the feudal economy evolved. The expansion of the nationwide market in China around the turn of the century undermined the self-sufficiency of the local economy. Modern trade was monopolized by the Blues. The Blacks remained economically weak and were discriminated against, which led to frequent armed clashes between the two groups. As the economy developed, the Blacks who had lived by themselves began to nurture closer contacts with the Han. Their specific manners and customs thus had been steadily receding over the last fifty to sixty years as they became assimilated by the Han.

The scholars thus concluded that the Blacks were Han who neither had dissolved their bonds to the maternal nationality nor had developed their own nationality. They had their peculiarities, but they did not have the characteristics of an independent nationality.[19]

Current problems of ethnic identification

The task of ethnic identification has still not been completed. A major reason for this is that since the late fifties the work has been dealt with rather dilatorily, and was even totally abandoned during the Cultural Revolution. In the late seventies, however, representatives of some ethnic groups called attention to this still unresolved problem, and the work was subsequently resumed. Encouraged by the political thaw, many groups whose recognition as independent nationalities had been rejected in the fifties re-petitioned for recognition; eighty groups totalling over 900,000 persons petitioned in the province of Guizhou alone,[20] including the Chuanqing.

Most of the applicants are smaller ethnic groups. These include:

—the "Pingwu-Tibetans" in the border region between Sichuan and Gansu, numbering a few thousand;[21]

—the Deng, a group of about 20,000 (1982) who live on the Chinese-Indian border;[22]

—the Laji, who numbered about 1,500 in 1982, from the Maguan district in Yunnan;[23]

—the Khmu, who are also in Laos, Thailand, and Vietnam, and who totaled about 2,100 in 1982;[24]

—the Mangren, who in 1982 amounted to 500 persons in four villages;

—the Hu, who in 1982 comprised 2,000 persons in the Autonomous Prefecture of Xishuangbanna of the Dai in the province of Yunnan;[25]

—about 25,000 Kucongs, stone-age hunters and gatherers who were first "discovered" in the 1950s in the forests of Yunnan;[26] and

—the Sherpas in Tibet, about 400 persons, who emigrated from Nepal about 300 years ago.[27]

Not all groups applied for recognition as nationalities by the time of the census in 1982. The Tuvins, for example, live in the Ili Autonomous Prefecture of the Kazak (Xinjiang Autonomous Region of the Uygur) in the Altai mountains on the Soviet border. In 1979, there were 166,000 Tuvin living in the Soviet Union. One hundred years ago, however, the members of this nationality living in China officially declared themselves Mongolians to avoid oppression by the then-ruling Qing dynasty, and to enjoy the favored status of the Mongolians, who were allies of the Manchurian court. In the 1982 population census the 2,600 Tuvins living in China were designated Mongolian and were so registered. At the time, scholars took note of the fact that this group spoke Mongolian with outsiders and had adopted many of the manners and customs of the surrounding Mongolian tribes, but spoke their own Turkic language among themselves.[28]

The population census discovered numerous new groups in other regions; in other cases, persons who had previously been classified as Han or another nationality applied for recognition as an ethnic minority. For instance:

—In the Hetian region in the south of the Xinjiang Autonomous Region, a village was found several days' ride into the desert whose inhabitants had hitherto been classified as Uygur, yet did not speak the

Uygur language. They used an Iranian language, which originally had been spoken by a people who had ruled over that region between the seventh and tenth centuries, but who later had been conquered and reduced to ruin in 1006 by the Islamic Kingdom of Kashgar.[29]

—In Yongdeng county (Gansu province), a village was found inhabited by 444 persons who were presumably gypsies.[30]

—In Yongtai county of Fujian, a group applied for recognition as Hui, although its members were no longer Moslem. They declared that they had previously been Hui during the Qing dynasty (1644–1911), but had been forced to abandon their faith. Although they had been gradually assimilated, they still retained a few of the Hui traditions, such as eating no pork for three days after the burial of kin.

—More than 2,000 Jews applied for recognition as an independent nationality, although both Chinese and Western scholars observed early in this century that Judaism was extinct in China. The application may very well have been made more for opportunist reasons (preference in admission examinations, hiring, and promotion on the basis of nationality status) than for reasons of actual group membership, since this group neither professes the Jewish faith nor do its members differ outwardly from the other Han Chinese.[31] In this case the Chinese government rejected recognition as a minority because of the "external political explosiveness" of the issue.

Chinese nationality policy in recent years has been more flexible with regard to naming minorities. Although discriminatory appellations for minorities (e.g., Luoluo with the pictograph "dog," or "pig" for the Yi) were permanently abolished by legislative decree in 1951,[32] most of the current names were fixed by the Han, and in many cases were adopted Han terms (the Yi call themselves Nuosu, but are called the Yi by the Han Chinese).

In recent years the minorities have been permitted more and more to determine the official names they go by. For example, the Benglong (a group of about 13,000 persons in the southwestern Chinese province of Yunnan) since 1985 are no longer known as "Benglong" but rather as "Deang," their term for themselves.[33]

The general liberalization that has ensued in the wake of reform is also reflected in the more flexible approach to granting the status of a minority. It is hoped that the discussion on this question will not be cut short, but will instead lead to a redefinition of the term that can then be further debated.

4

Autonomy and the Right to Self-Administration on Trial

The Chinese call the policy of regional autonomy the nucleus of their minority policy. Let us therefore examine the theoretical and practical aspects of this policy.

What does autonomy mean?

Minorities have enjoyed an autonomy (*zizhi*) defined by territory and nationality since the fifties. At that time, regions inhabited by one or several minorities were united into a single administrative unit (be it autonomous region, autonomous prefecture, autonomous county, or autonomous township) and bodies of self-administration were established. In 1989, there existed 141 areas with regional national autonomy (five autonomous regions at the provincial level: Inner Mongolia, Xinjiang of the Uygur, Guangxi of the Zhuang, Tibet, and Ningxia of the Hui; 31 autonomous prefectures and 105 autonomous counties or banners, as they are called in Inner Mongolia). In the same years there were also nearly 3,000 nationality townships.[1] Together, the autonomous administrative regions in 1987 covered a total area of 6.1 million square kilometers (64 percent of the area of the country) and comprised a population of 142.5 million people, including more than 62.5 million members of national minorities.

Autonomy does not mean that these regions have the right to secede from the sovereign territory of the People's Republic of China, but it does mean that, under the "direction of higher authorities," they enjoy certain special rights over other administrative units. In these regions, the language(s) and writing(s) of the region's autonomous nationality (or nationalities) should be used; administration must (or should) be in the hands of functionaries from the minority population; the regions can promulgate their own laws and regulations, draw up their own production plans (within the bounds of the central state plan), and choose their own path of economic and cultural development (within the lines of the constitution). Furthermore, the autonomous regions can administer local finances themselves (within the framework of financial planning for the state as a whole), and can have their own local security forces.

A few basic rights were established for minorities by edict in the fifties that concerned the practical implementation of regional autonomy, protection of the rights of dispersed minorities, financial rights, equal rights for all nationalities, etc.[2] But since the 1954 constitution did not provide sufficient constitutional guarantee for these rights,[3] they basically did not exist. The periods of political radicalism (the Great Leap Forward, the Cultural Revolution) demonstrated that the general policy being pursued was one of assimilating minorities, with the intensity depending on the political climate. This policy, coupled with the effects of the Cultural Revolution, gave rise to considerable unrest in the minority regions. Adding to this, the 1978 constitution did not even grant minorities the rights that they had been given under the 1954 constitution.

The minorities' discontent erupted at the third session of the National People's Congress (the Chinese parliament) in September 1980, when heavy criticisms, proposals, and demands from minority delegates were for the first time presented to the public in the daily press.[4] These concessions must be seen from the perspective that the minorities have effectively enjoyed no more than mere paper autonomy since the fifties. A Li representative from the island of Hainan lamented the uncertainty that had hitherto reigned about minorities' legal status:

> There were laws for national minorities as early as the fifties. But in 1958 they were criticized and the Autonomous Prefecture of Hainan of the Li and Miao was dissolved. In 1962 it was reinstated. In 1966 it was once again declared that autonomous regions were no longer necessary. Later the autonomous prefecture was once more reinstat-

ed. Today a party secretary comes and abolishes it, tomorrow comes another one and restores it again. Often the autonomous region and its development depend on the attitude of this or that leader or this or that course.[5]

On top of this, when the province of Hainan was established in 1988, the Autonomous Prefecture of the Li and Miao was dissolved once again.

(The Chinese leadership became aware of the threat lurking under the surface of minority discontent. In 1981, a Han Chinese official in Xinjiang complained that the Uygur would tell him repeatedly: "What difference does it make to us if the Russians come. They'll cut off the heads of the Han, not ours"—a sign of how much some members of ethnic minorities had already become alienated from the Han.)

In 1980, minority representatives demanded an immediate realization and extension of regional autonomy in all domains. At the center of the discussion was the question of legal guarantees for, and the rights to, self-administration. The 1982 constitution upgraded the role of minorities and in general gave them more rights then they had ever had before.[6] At the same time the Chinese leadership promised that the relevant paragraphs in the constitution would be set down in legislation[7] to cover the minorities' economic and cultural development as well as to provide broad powers of self-determination over natural resources and development (albeit within the Chinese constitution).[8] The subsequent "law of regional autonomy of the nationalities of the People's Republic of China" of 1984, based on the corresponding articles of the 1982 constitution, serves as a guideline for all legislation for ethnic minorities.[9] Compared to other regulations since 1949, the new law provides distinctly broader rights of self-administration, and defines more specifically the functions and rights of certain administrative bodies, as well as outlines the interrelations between bodies of self-administration and higher authorities of the state. Leading officials must now be members of the nationality (nationalities) exercising autonomy (Table 4.1 shows the proportion of minority population in units' population); resolutions and instructions from higher political organs that do not take into consideration the conditions in an autonomous unit need not unconditionally be implemented. The autonomous units receive broader rights—for regional planning, economic development, protection, and administration of their resources, foreign trade, the financial and tax sectors, education, health, etc.—than do other areas. As for relations between the autonomous unit and the state, the state is committed to provide support and assistance.

The Communist Party of China considers a set of legal instruments sufficient protection for the rights of minorities. But Chinese experience has shown that during periods of ideological and political radicalization, laws and legal decrees quickly lose their force. The "laws" therefore offer no legal security, at least as long as the Communist Party stands above the law. The events of the spring of 1989 exemplified that fundamental changes in the field of law are not possible without fundamental changes in the political system. All previous pronouncements that no one—including a party leader or the party itself—would be considered above the law were proven to be just empty promises.

The autonomy law of 1984 is the most far-reaching legislation to date on the rights of ethnic minorities. Autonomous units are empowered to enact laws that give legislative guarantees for minorities' customs and traditions, edcucation, language and writing, marriage laws, etc. The law represents an official upgrading of minorities, their autonomy, and their self-administrative bodies. However, at its core the law is subject to the power monopoly of the Communist Party. If this monopoly cannot be broken, then real autonomy is not possible, and every attempt by a nationality to attain more independence will be considered an attack and thus will be suppressed. For that reason, laws are ineffectual because they remain subordinate to the party's claim for political power, and thereby leave the minority population subject to the despotism and arbitrary wills of authorities and functionaries.

Formally, the 1984 law grants the autonomous units more rights. But evaluation of the law reveals that the clauses are formulated in such general terms that the law is ineffectual without supplemental and substantial legislation. They may provide guidelines for future legislative regulations, but for now their legislative bark is stronger than their bite.

Table 4.1

Proportion of Ethnic Minorities in Autonomous Administrative Units

In autonomous administrative units of each region

Region	(1985)			(1987)		
	Total population	Ethnic minority population	Percentage	Total population	Ethnic minority population	Percentage
Hebei	239,000	53,000	22.2	1,094,000	509,000	46.5
Inner Mongolia	20,066,700	3,296,200	16.4	20,536,000	3,595,400	17.5
Liaoning	2,440,500	1,189,000	48.7	2,460,900	1,196,000	48.6
Jilin	2,570,000	878,000	34.2	2,635,300	917,300	34.8
Heilongjiang	220,000	40,000	18.2	227,000	36,000	15.9
Zhejiang	166,100	16,700	10.1	168,800	17,000	10.1
Hubei	3,977,500	1,642,700	41.3	4,094,500	1,690,600	41.3
Hunan	3,799,300	2,460,500	64.8	4,457,200	2,880,800	64.6
Guangdong	2,407,500	980,400	40.7	2,475,100	1,022,900	41.3
Guangxi	38,729,500	15,098,900	39.0	40,164,000	15,721,000	39.1
Sichuan	7,640,800	3,930,400	51.4	7,828,500	4,023,400	51.4
Guizhou	10,907,200	5,644,800	51.8	12,624,400	6,622,700	52.5
Yunnan	17,522,100	9,089,500	51.9	18,026,200	9,446,600	52.4
Tibet	1,993,800	1,922,900	96.4	2,079,500	1,984,500	95.4
Gansu	2,471,300	1,302,700	52.1	2,542,200	1,350,000	53.1
Qinghai	2,568,400	1,372,100	53.4	2,638,000	1,441,100	54.6
Ningxia	4,146,000	1,348,800	32.5	4,351,600	1,433,000	32.9
Xinjiang	13,611,400	8,262,100	60.7	14,063,300	8,633,500	61.4
Total	135,477,100	58,528,700	43.2	142,466,500	62,525,800	43.9

Source: Zhongguo tongji nianjian (1986), p. 79, and idem (1988), p. 84.

Autonomy and economic development

The minority regions are among the poorest and least-developed regions in China, primarily for historical reasons. A major portion of the peoples in these regions were driven back into desolate and inhospitable regions by the Han and isolated themselves so as not to be overrun by the steadily growing, land-poor Han population.

The development policy of the sixties and seventies, in itself a complete failure, failed to bring the envisaged progress to these areas. The central government is currently making an effort to "develop" the minority regions, but the minorities themselves view this with mixed feelings. While the minorities desire progress and modernization, at the same time they are apprehensive of the consequences of such progress.

At present there is a high level of anxiety in many minority regions about the economic "opening" of these regions.[10] Considerable fear still remains that the minorities and their regions might suffer major harm, find their resources plundered, and see their national and cultural identities lost. The Uygur complain of the influx of innumerable Han to develop the deposits of raw material in that region; Xinjiang and Inner Mongolia have seen demonstrations during the last few years against the population influx and ecological destruction by factories or individuals from the Han regions. This indicates an undercurrent of unrest among many minorities. The rebellions in Tibet in the last few years and the separatist tendencies in Xinjiang[11] are a further sign that the discontent is increasing in minority regions.

While the state and the larger minorities have a legitimate interest in developing the minority regions and in utilizing their resources, the minorities are apprehensive of being inundated by the Han. Some of the smaller groups would like to remain isolated, preserving their traditional way of life. The Han Chinese complaint that a "commodity economy" has not developed in these areas and that the inhabitants are not interested in "production for the market" has little impact on these peoples. Progress is therefore often rigorously imposed from above, in some cases with the help of minority functionaries. It is true that the higher authorities show little indulgence when matters of economic development are concerned. Regional and local authorities have only a slight comprehension of minorities' interests in preserving their culture, lifestyle, and traditions. Thus there is a risk that the cultures of minor ethnic groups, who are unable to defend themselves, will be destroyed—something that scarcely anyone considered when these territories were opened up.

The lower administrative levels (provinces, prefectures, enterprises), however, acquired broader decision-making powers under the economic reform after 1979. Actual local conditions were to be used as the initial framework for economic development. Autonomous regions were permitted to make their own decisions concerning the development and exploitation of their resources, which were to be used to benefit the local population. The minority regions as well acquired a greater say in these matters and profited from the general economic boom of the last few years—for instance, in 1986 the state allocated 8.5 billion *yuan* for the development of their economies. Despite this, in 1988, 29 percent of the minority population did not have adequate food and clothing,[12] and about 25 percent of the population earning less than the living wage belonged to ethnic minorities.[13]

The gap between minority and Han regions is growing.[14] Eastern China, which is already more developed, has better conditions for economic growth (more integrated infrastructures, proximity to the coast, relatively well-developed industrial centers, technology, skilled manpower, etc.). It has the most foreign contacts and receives the lion's share of aid from Western countries. If the state is unable to guarantee a broad margin of self-determination to minorities' autonomy in matters of economic development, while at the same time allowing them to preserve their cultural identity, nationality conflicts will become more acute as time goes on.

"Unhealthy" and "healthy" customs

From the 1950s on, a distinction was drawn between "healthy" and "unhealthy" manners and customs, with "unhealthy" customs to be abolished and "healthy" ones retained. Since these terms were never elucidated, intrusion on customs and habits at a local level became a regular occurrence. The authorities routinely measured local customs against Han Chinese standards. Initiation rites, love feasts, and youth houses in which unmarried boys and girls could meet and practice "free love," were regularly prohibited because they ran against Han notions of morality.

Customs, manners, and festivities were restored in the early eighties. The constitution states explicitly, "[All nationalities] are free to retain or to reform their manners and customs."[15] In 1986, however, *Liangshan bao*, the bilingual (Yi and Chinese) newspaper in the Autonomous Prefecture of Liangshan, reported on the prohibition of premature-death solemnities for surviving parents.[16] In this traditional observance, all the relatives and friends came together bringing gifts, and took part in a common feast lasting several days. The prohibition was imposed by the regional government on the grounds of "extravagance," even though the peasants consumed only what was theirs and used their own money; it is not difficult to imagine the feelings provoked by this prohibition. Since the local authorities consider themselves the representatives of local minorities, however, members of minorities have no chance to defend themselves against such decisions.

In another instance in 1986, a top official of the State's Nationality Commission had the showcases on the topic "religion" removed a few days before the opening of an exhibition on the Li on Hainan Island because "superstitious things" were being demonstrated. By the next day, all that was left of the showcase was a photo depicting the prime minister on a visit to Hainan.

The uncertainty and fear perceptible in attitudes and measures concerning minority customs may derive from the Confucian contempt for the former "barbarians," from the fear of possible political missteps, and from a low level of education, and extends into every level of the bureaucracy. Thus, a Va cadre dismissed the question about the headhunting formerly practiced by the Va with the exculpation that the practice had earlier been "forced upon us by the Guomindang of Chiang Kai-shek." This illustrates that many minority cadres have no innate sense of the customs and usages of their nationality, whose rationale and historical context they do not understand. But the fault does not lie solely with them: they have been told for decades that their ethnic customs were backward, offensive, and reactionary.

As long as there are no definitive legal guarantees of the right and freedom to retain or reform customs and mores, it will always be easy for some functionary to brand some particular custom "reactionary," "obscene," or "obstructive of production," and thereby prohibit it. A

Table 4.2

Ethnic Minorities by Level of Education (1982)

Nationality	Persons over six years old	Students	Completed university	Attended			Illiterate or semiliterate
				Upper secondary school	Lower secondary school	Elementary school	
Han	889,788,266	1,609,288	4,427,991	66,529,262	178,197,388	355,346,694	237,720,787
Total minorities	57,164,045	66,293	184,673	3,055,370	8,221,284	20,304,276	25,332,149
Mongolian	2,901,378	8,927	18,796	270,898	573,857	1,163,855	865,045
Hui	6,255,819	12,457	37,709	458,728	1,203,595	1,894,442	2,648,888
Tibetan	3,234,569	1,930	5,850	38,497	127,985	635,597	2,424,710
Uygur	4,976,966	6,849	12,676	208,310	613,336	1,967,410	1,168,385
Miao	4,222,388	1,436	4,481	97,153	358,912	1,241,057	2,519,349
Yi	4,548,532	1,278	3,157	66,089	328,164	1,273,588	2,874,256
Zhuang	11,363,110	6,987	22,353	708,519	1,846,807	4,947,176	3,831,268
Bouyei	1,806,302	837	2,082	37,051	184,294	562,490	1,019,548
Korean	1,585,769	8,193	26,382	323,837	541,681	502,695	182,981
Manchu	3,774,872	8,475	29,164	393,934	997,384	1,648,214	697,701
Dong	1,234,125	878	2,127	42,986	150,275	479,318	558,541
Yao	1,178,987	444	1,542	42,778	109,113	457,004	568,106
Bai	976,670	1,373	3,268	40,693	144,351	380,465	406,520
Tujia	2,506,000	928	3,488	133,790	399,423	1,123,936	844,435
Hani	873,391	132	330	9,076	50,703	190,526	622,624
Kazak	725,130	1,483	2,547	41,599	124,781	351,272	203,448
Dai	723,118	309	546	10,092	51,108	244,554	416,509
Li	725,804	453	907	37,001	97,861	257,977	331,605
Lisu	397,426	94	324	3,336	17,829	86,434	289,409
Va	246,439	39	153	2,317	13,737	58,873	171,320
She	323,665	157	435	8,707	27,787	124,860	161,719
Gaoshan	1,517	12	48	262	421	480	294
Lahu	252,243	29	76	1,188	6,867	35,438	208,645

48

Group							
Shui	237,660	98	204	4,103	18,714	63,953	150,588
Dongxiang	240,999	75	94	1,768	6,551	20,817	211,694
Naxi	221,035	335	943	10,784	36,545	85,212	87,216
Jingpo	76,058	40	100	864	4,867	22,688	47,499
Kirgiz	91,726	107	302	4,261	10,533	38,129	38,394
Tu	133,589	230	458	3,505	12,831	37,695	78,870
Daur	80,546	395	1,096	9,916	22,147	31,218	15,774
Mulam	76,900	88	185	4,649	11,087	33,571	27,320
Qiang	84,915	130	171	3,644	10,033	29,638	41,299
Bulang	48,067	13	20	395	2,001	9,599	36,039
Salar	54,830	97	180	1,108	3,623	9,757	40,065
Maonan	32,157	46	114	2,659	5,332	13,859	10,147
Gelo	44,351	17	53	753	4,306	14,126	25,096
Xibe	71,924	400	904	9,484	21,247	30,589	9,300
Pumi	20,440	9	36	362	1,789	5,524	12,720
Achang	16,982	20	16	263	1,066	5,298	10,319
Tajik	21,620	22	65	859	2,500	7,695	10,479
Nu	18,529	7	45	420	1,733	4,407	11,917
Uzbek	10,261	81	216	1,276	2,435	4,104	2,149
Russian	2,643	18	56	397	824	850	498
Ewenki	16,280	76	129	1,673	4,057	7,383	2,962
Deang	10,043	4	9	69	346	2,250	7,365
Bonan	7,997	6	22	188	467	1,145	6,169
Yugur	9,090	19	37	413	1,030	3,738	3,853
Jing	11,289	37	64	805	1,650	4,830	3,903
Tatar	3,359	38	130	480	842	1,372	497
Drung	3,717	6	15	89	296	944	2,367
Oroqen	3,434	15	47	389	988	1,414	581
Hezhen	1,255	11	27	238	343	437	199
Moinba	988	1	15	25	106	415	426
Lhoba	926	—	7	11	39	223	646
Jinuo	10,495	9	13	141	775	4,148	5,409
Other	660,883	126	358	10,150	59,134	178,356	412,759

Source: Zhongguo 1982 nian renkou pucha ziliao (1985), pp. 240ff.

49

precise specification of which customs should be reformed and which should not has never been forthcoming; the definitions are too variable, the interpretations too diverse. And whose standard should be applied? Surely not that of the Han: criteria such as "to the benefit or in the interest of the reactionary ruling classes" or "obstructive of the development of the economy and culture" can be interpreted in too many ways. Autonomous administrative units should be allowed to decide on these questions themselves and make their own regulations free of outside interference. These decisions cannot be made by officials (who are more inclined to decide against a custom rather than for it), but must rather be the result of open and candid discussion within the nationality itself.

Problems of the education system

Since a large number of specialized and skilled workers are necessary for building the economies in the minorities regions, and since skilled Han workers are reluctant to move to these areas, skilled workers must be trained from among the local population. However, the standards of minority education are usually very low (see Table 4.2). "Nationality schools," in which the language of the local minority or minorities is the language of instruction, have been restored or new ones established in recent years in minority regions. Children from ethnic minorities may study in these nationality schools at state expense until they complete the upper level of secondary school, which allows them to take part in the universities' admission examinations. The schools' training helps to increase the quota of minority students among college and university students—from 4.2 percent in 1978 to 6.1 percent in 1987— but it remains below the proportion of minorities (8.0 percent) in the total population.[17] The rate of illiteracy of people between the ages of 12 and 50 is, according to official data, about 44.3 percent (as compared to all of China at about 20 percent) and in some places is as high as 80 percent.[18]

In the upper grades of the nationality schools, however, instruction is often in Han Chinese because there are only a few textbooks available in the minority languages (due to shortages of materials and money) and no local teaching personnel. Functionaries and the narrow stratum of intellectuals of minority origin actually prefers that their children attend Han schools and speak Chinese because in institutions of higher education (with the exception of a few in Xinjiang, Inner Mongolia, Tibet, and some other regions) Chinese is the language of instruction just as it is in administrative seats and in the cities. Specialized training and advanced training therefore require a higher level of competence in Han language than in a person's own native minority language. This does not mean that there is no conflict about the lack of training in minority languages, however.

Minority applicants do have advantages over Han applicants in higher education. Many universities have set up courses to help prepare minority applicants for the examinations, for which their passing grade is lower than for Han. Eleven Nationalities Institutes (*minzu xueyuan*— special universities) offer specialized courses for students from minority regions if they agree to return to their region. Admission is based on a quota system of so many persons of each nationality.

Since members of ethnic minorities should be given priority in admission to institutions of higher learning as well as in hiring and promotion, Han Chinese have attempted in recent years to register their children in minority regions through illegal means, including bribery and connections, and have them declared members of national minorities. They also submit falsified proof that their ancestors were members of minorities.[19] Thus members of ethnic minorities are not disadvantaged in higher education; on the contrary, often they are favored. But as a result of their education in a Han Chinese environment and the Han Chinese language, they become partially sinified. A large number of minority students educated after 1966 have either no or only very little knowledge of their oral or written language (with the exception of those from the major groups with full-fledged written languages such as the Uygur, Tibetans, Mongolians, and Koreans). In Guizhou, a multinationality province, 35 percent of all members of ethnic minorities no longer speak their original language, but speak only Han Chinese.[20]

There is a danger that the future upper stratum of minorities will no longer know their own ethnic language and will spurn their own ethnic group. Culture and language would then continue to exist only in peasant regions, and would no longer develop. A rise in the level of education would come to mean an increased assimilation and sinification of the minority populations, and a decreased level of identity for these people.

How is autonomy for ethnic minorities
to be assessed?

In China, autonomy means autonomy within a unitary state. The relationship between the central and lower levels is defined by the principle of "democratic centralism." According to party statutes, this means subordination of the individual to the organization, subordination of the minority to the majority, subordination of the lower levels to the higher levels, and finally subordination of the whole party to the central committee.[21] Because of this, autonomous regions have to adapt to this overall union and are not allowed to declare their withdrawal, although the various nationalities do formally enjoy equality of status. In this scheme, autonomy is subject to the interest of both the state and the Communist Party of China. The constitution (which *inter alia* implies adherence to the socialist system) and precepts of the state at large are binding for all nationalities. Within this scope, the nationalities are theoretically entitled to make their own decisions on development concepts—that is, with approval from above. This approval requirement is in effect a safeguard against a region or minority in one way or another pulling out of the union. Thus autonomy is severely restricted from the very outset.

The autonomy law of 1984 enumerates and demarcates the respective powers and responsibilities of the state and subordinate political entities. But autonomous administrative entities are subject to other administrative bodies, which are themselves completely under Han control because they are subordinate to central bodies in Beijing or to provinces where the Han are in the majority. This would be less of a problem if the relations between the state and the autonomous entities were defined by law and if they functioned in that way. While autonomous regions are directly under the central authorities, intermediate levels are interposed for autonomous prefectures and counties. In these instances, a general and enumerative definition of responsibilities should also be necessary to outline statutory control functions (e.g., independent courts to deal with competence disputes between autonomous administrative units and higher level authorities) and political control functions (e.g., in the party and government organizations).

A greater degree of autonomy also requires a broad separation between party and state apparatus. As long as the Communist Party can claim absolute power, and as long as party instructions can contravene government decisions at every level as well as laws themselves, a legal vagueness prevails and autonomy can at any moment be abolished. Thus, a detailed separation of powers among party, state, and judicial bodies is vital. But, as was shown above, such measures are purely cosmetic as long as the fundamental character of the political system does not change. Even small changes in this respect can encounter major resistance within the party, given the loss of (usually personal) power change entails. It is also difficult for local governments of autonomous units to break the habit of kowtowing to local party organizations. Thus laws alone are not sufficient to ensure any notable degree of independence in decision-making. Other supervisory bodies and, above all, changes in the political and administrative structure of China are also required.

There remains the touchy question of "the members of ethnic minorities living scattered" throughout the country. Approximately 11 million members of national minorities (roughly one-sixth of the total) live outside the autonomous regions in "mixed" regions; another 5.7 million have no autonomy because of their relatively sparse settlement patterns. Since these 18.7 million enjoy no effective autonomy, it is doubly difficult for them to lay claim to any rights at all, let alone to realize them.

5

Development of a Multinational Province:
The Yunnan Case

China's most recent reform and development policy has attracted attention from around the world. Reform measures that break with the rigid economic model borrowed in the fifties from the Soviet Union are causing a radical restructuring of the Chinese economy. Greater freedom is being giving to market factors and private initiative, so-called "Special Economic Zones" have been set up that enjoy special economic conditions, and the door has been opened to foreign capital—all in the hope that these measures will bring life to the Chinese economy. However, experience is showing that even though a political program has been ratified in Beijing, its implementation in the provinces is not necessarily smooth and problem-free. The following sections illustrate the practical problems that centrally ratified reforms can cause for the provinces, using as an example the southwestern, multinational province of Yunnan. Yunnan is one of the poorest provinces of China and, despite abundant natural resources, is burdened by an unfavorable terrain and location. A development program tailored specifically to the region is therefore especially needed here.

The state of economic development of Yunnan
at the end of the 1970s

There are three factors that set Yunnan apart from most of the other Chinese provinces: it is a border region with a 4,000 km border; it has 94 percent mountains and highlands; and it is host to 24 ethnic minorities that make up about one-third of the population (see Table 5.1).[1]

Map 5.1. **Administrative Divisions and Nationalities in the Province of Yunnan.**

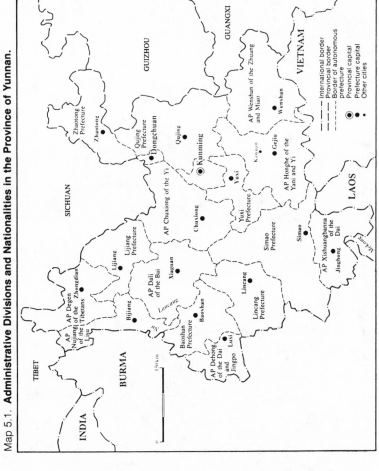

Source: Geographische Rundschau 3 (1986).

Note: AP—Autonomous Prefecture.

56

Map 5.2. **Cultivated Areas, Industrial Localities, and Natural Resources in Yunnan.**

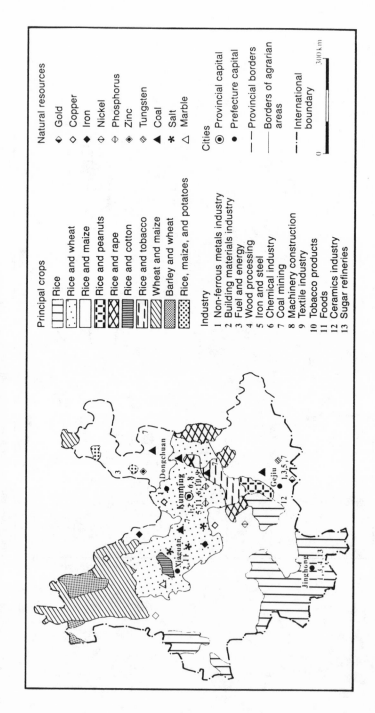

Source: *Geographische Rundschau* 3 (1986).

Table 5.1

Yunnan's National Minorities (1985)
(total Yunnan population = 34.1 million)

	% of total
Han Chinese	68.1
Yi	10.2
Bai	3.4
Hani	3.3
Zhuang	2.7
Dai	2.6
Miao	2.3
Lisu	1.5
Hui	1.3
Lahu	1.0
Va	0.9
Naxi	0.7
Yao	0.5
Tibetan	0.3
Jingpo	0.3
Other	0.9

Source: Yunnan tongji nianjin (1987), 26.

Map 5.1 illustrates the distribution of the Han and minorities in the province.

Abundant natural resources (especially non-ferrous metals), vast water-power and energy potential, and tropical crops and precious woods are actually favorable starting conditions for economic development (see Map 5.2). Yet in 1981 Yunnan ranked third lowest among the provinces in terms of gross industrial and agricultural products, with a per capita output of 407 *yuan* (compared with 757 for China as a whole) (see Figure 5.1). Its per capita agricultural output was only 69.7 percent of the national average, and per capita industrial output was even lower at 40.3 percent.

The increase in its gross output between 1949 and 1980 was 7.1 percent, also notably under the national average of 9.5 percent. Measured against the national average, Yunnan's share declined in all economic sectors (see Tables 5.2 and 5.3).[2]

Figure 5.1. **Industrialization of Chinese Administrative Regions (persons employed in industry per 1000 inhabitants).**

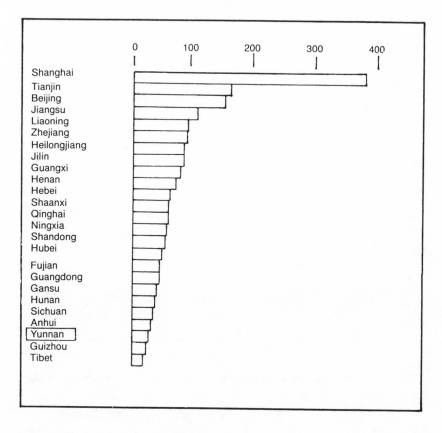

Reasons for the development lag

A review of past growth strategies shows that the party leadership in Beijing and likewise in Yunnan ordered the implementation of plans that ignored specific local conditions; one such plan was in the area of crop cultivation policy.

In the early 1960s, the party leadership called for an increase in grain cultivation in China, with the original goal to have provinces self-sufficient in grain supply. By the late sixties, however, the rigid application of this policy had resulted in the concentration the agriculture almost

Table 5.2

Economic Growth of Yunnan Compared with China Overall

Year	Industrial and agricultural (GOV) Proportion of national GOV (%)	Placement*	Industrial GOV Proportion of national GOV (%)	Placement*	Agricultural GOV Proportion of national GOV (%)	Placement*	Grain Proportion of total national yield (%)	Placement*	National income Proportion of total national income (%)	Placement*	Per capita consumption (yuan) Yunnan	China
1949	2.4	—	1.3	—	2.8	—	3.5	—	—	—	—	—
1952	1.7	—	—	—	2.2	—	—	—	1.8	—	51	76
1957	2.0	—	1.4	21	2.7	—	3.0	16	2.3	—	76	102
1965	1.9	19	1.3	22	3.2	16	3.0	14	1.9	—	94	125
1975	1.7	22	1.3	22	3.0	16	2.8	—	—	—	130	158
1980	1.5	23	1.2	23	2.5	16	2.7	15	2.0	—	173	227
1985	1.5	22	1.5	22	2.0	19	2.5	17	2.1	20	308	407

Sources: Zhongguo tongji nianjian (1986), pp. 40ff; Yunnan tongji nianjian (1986), pp. 6ff.

Note: GOV = gross output value.

*Among all 29 administrative divisions at provincial level.

Table 5.3

Comparative Figures for Economic Sectors (1985)

	Yunnan	China	Yunnan's autonomous areas
Share of population	3.26%	100%	
Per capita output value (industry)	368 yuan	838 yuan	195 yuan
(agriculture)	233 yuan	438 yuan	234 yuan
Per capita gross output value	849 yuan	1,560 yuan	429 yuan
National income per capita	423 yuan	653 yuan	
Cash income of peasants per capita	338 yuan	398 yuan	
Per capita labor productivity of state-owned industry	12,789 yuan	15,198 yuan	
Share in gross agricultural output value	41.6%	34.3%	54.5%
Share in gross industrial output value	58.4%	65.7%	45.5%
Grain yield per hectare	188 kg	232 kg	
Machine-cultivated area	5.9%	35.3%	
Per capita grain yield	274 kg	363 kg	271 kg
Per capita cultivated area	0.08 hectare	0.09 hectare	0.09 hectare

Sources: *Zhongguo tongji nianjian* (1986), pp. 40ff; *Yunnan tongji nianjian* (1986), pp. 6ff.

exclusively on grain, with the consequent abandonment of traditional crop structures, not infrequently under protest from the local population.

In Yunnan's Xishuangbanna Autonomous Prefecture of the Dai, the traditional agrarian structures had been in forestry and in raising livestock, fruit, and tropical crops. Slash-and-burn cultivation was and still is the most widespread form for clearing new areas for crop cultivation in this prefecture, although few areas needed to be cleared for cultivation because of the emphasis on forestry. Slash-and-burn cultivation, however, drains the soil of nutrients so that it is unusable for years. When the prefecture switched over to grain production, fields made tillable by slash-and-burn cultivation yielded an average of 135 kg of grain per mu (= 1/15 ha) in the first year, 65 kg in the second, 50 kg in the third, and only 5 kg in the fourth. Within three years the soil was completely depleted and new land had to be cleared—with the same result.

As more and more land was cleared, the forest area shrank drastically. Whereas in 1950 Xishuangbanna still was 69 percent forest area, by 1981 it was only 30 percent. Consequently, wood products, which formerly had been the most important commercial good, became almost totally unavailable. Soil erosion, the depletion of water sources, climatic changes, frequent crop diseases, and pests were further consequences of the slash-and-burn cultivation.[3]

In addition to the grave damage caused by this policy, the state crop cultivation policy also caused agricultural output as a whole to decline. For instance, in 1957 Yunnan province exported 43,000 tons of grain to other provinces; by 1977 it had to import 180,000 tons. While the growth in population played some role in this, the decisive factor was the abortive economic policy of the 1970s, as the following example makes evident.

In 1970 the Yunnan party committee decided that 70 percent of the harvest from the first spring planting had to be a new high-yield rice variety that had been tested in northern China; 70 percent of the second spring planting was then to produce wheat. In every district the fulfillment or nonfulfillment of this arbitrarily set target became a question of "political attitude" toward the policy of "concentrate on the cultivation of wheat."[4] The peasants had to pull up rice that had been already planted and replace it with the new variety of "high-yield, round-grain rice." But because of the weather situation, the lack of fertilizers, and the peasants' lack of experience with this rice variety, the yield declined drastically. To meet the target of 70 percent wheat, the latter was planted on quickly drained, terraced fields, with the result again being a poor harvest and, in some parts of the province, even famine.

The development of single-crop agriculture (see Table 5.4) also handicapped light industry, 80 percent of which is based on raw materials from agriculture, causing constrictions in supplies.[5] Thus a policy whose aim was to introduce a unified development program for the whole country was doomed to miscarry, and it ended in a general economic crisis.

Reform policy

Chinese economists were aware even in 1978 that the economic crisis would not be overcome without fundamental reform of the overcentral-

Table 5.4

Share of the Different Agricultural Branches in Total Yunnan Agrarian Production (%)

	1978	1980	1982	1984	1985
Farming	66.6	64.6	62.1	60.2	57.5
Forestry	5.7	6.4	7.3	9.7	10.4
Livestock	16.4	16.3	19.6	21.1	21.4
Peasant cottage industries (handicrafts, sideline production)	11.5	12.7	10.7	8.7	10.3
Fisheries	0.2	0.2	0.3	0.3	0.4
Total	100.0	100.0	100.0	100.0	100.0

Source: Yunnan tongji nianjian (1986), p. 190/f.

ized economic system. The 1979 reform was intended to provide a new emphasis on the regional level as well as to create the preconditions necessary to implement suitable development strategies such as diversification in agriculture, greater autonomy for regions and producers, the creation of rural industries, and the development of small cities.

Rural Reform

The first step was agricultural reform. The 1979 reforms transferred the right to use the land to individual households on a contractual basis. Villages and counties also acquired broader powers to make their own decisions about crop structure and the development of different agrarian sectors. Against this background, the Yunnan peasants' incomes and returns from agriculture rose considerably, although the income gap relative to the national average widened (see Table 5.5).

A rise in income is not merely the consequence of more intensive cultivation but also of a more varied intra-family division of labor. Lucun township provides a good example of this: in 1982 the farmers calculated that 270 of a total of 477 available laborers would be enough to cultivate the 1,266 mu (about 85 ha) tillable land. A figure of 4.6 mu per worker was considered efficient and on the whole feasible. Therefore, 120 workers left the agrarian sector in early 1983 and established five construction brigades, and 51 others started small manufacturing

Table 5.5

Peasant Living Standards

	1978	1982	1983	1984	1985
1. Per capita peasant income (in *yuan*)					
Yunnan	124	232	267	310	338
China	134	270	310	355	398
Yunnan compared with national average (%)	93	86	86	87	85
2. Grain consumption of peasants (in pounds)					
Yunnan	365	460	463	470	452
China	496	520	520	533	515
Yunnan compared with national average (%)	74	88	89	88	88

Source: Zhongguo tongji nianjian (1986), pp. 677–679.

concerns or businesses (the other 36 had not yet found new jobs). In families whose income from farming was lower than from any other activity, the new occupations became the principal source of earnings. These households gave back the land they had received on a contractual basis, and specialized in other vocations.[6]

In early 1984, a total of 10.5 percent of all peasant households in Yunnan were "special households" of this type, incorporating a broad range of occupations (see Table 5.6).[7] Such specialization furthered the restructuring of the province's agrarian sector, the diversification of the economy, and the expansion of commodity production. An indication of this change in the local economy was that only 40 percent of the province's agricultural output reached the market in 1984; 60 percent was consumed by the peasants themselves. By comparison, in China as a whole 53.3 percent was sent to market.[8]

The overall plan is to create more small cities by expanding the rural non-agricultural sector and rural cooperative and private industries. These cities are to function as local centers of production and as market centers, occupying an intermediate position between the village and mid- and large-sized cities. A shift in the location of industry (from the cities to rural areas) is also intended. The estimates are that 5–6 million

Table 5.6

Specialized Households in the Countryside in Yunnan (1984)

Sector	Number of farms	% of all households
Plant cultivation	229,322	40.3
Livestock-raising and fisheries	164,267	28.8
Processing industry	49,106	8.6
Trade and services	52,681	9.2
Transportation	31,867	5.6
Developmental and reclamation activity (land, mines, waterways)	2,492	0.4
Agrarian technology	8,139	1.6
Others	31,989	5.6

Source: *Yunnan shehui kexue* 4 (1984), pp. 6–7.

rural workers will leave the agricultural sector and move to the small cities by the year 2000.[9]

The development of small cities is especially important in this province since its urbanization ratio in 1985 was only 14 percent (China's as a whole at that time was 23.5 percent); in minority regions it is even below 10 percent.[10]

But lack of capital, a deficient infrastructure, and the political conservatism of local officials are obstacles to reform. A 1984 study in the autonomous prefecture of Chuxiong, one of the more-developed regions of Yunnan, showed that many peasants were still apprehensive of larger incomes because they are an irritation to local functionaries. Fear of change in political climate continues. Thus the specialization of peasant households, too, has not kept pace with the country as a whole.[11]

The income growth has not developed consistently in Yunnan: only 1,128 specialized plots (0.2 percent of all such individual plots) earned more than 10,000 *yuan* per year in 1984 (an average peasant income was 301 *yuan* in that same year). Thus a small portion of the peasantry has profited from the reform more than others.[12] A study in Caobazhai township, which is representative of Yunnan, showed that of the 40 households there, only one earned more than 200 *yuan* per year in 1984, 18 earned between 100 and 199 *yuan*, and 21 earned less than 100 *yuan*.[13] Income differentials are also growing among the regions, since regions with more advantageous natural conditions and better infrastructures are developing more rapidly than those without them.

Urban reform

The first reform attempts in Yunnan began in February 1979 in the cities, initially in a series of pilot plants. The following were envisioned:

—greater autonomy for enterprises (including the right to keep part of their profits; the right to use those parts for expanding their production, for intra-enterprise social services, and for bonuses);

—indicative planning and expanding market elements (allowing products in excess of the plan to be sold independently; possibly having a choice in the purchase of raw materials);

—internal decision-making powers (introduction of pay based on performance and regular responsibilities) and a say for the workforce in internal matters ("workers and Staff Congresses").[14]

But the results remained modest when measured against the country as a whole. Although the number of state enterprises operating at a loss diminished, the overall loss increased.[15] The ineffectiveness of the reforms up to the mid-eighties when compared with other provinces is evident in the following example from Kunming, the provincial capital. In early 1985, there were 300,000 pairs of locally produced leather shoes sitting unwanted in stock—all of them obsolete models. Whereas suppliers from outside the province were able to take advantage of the new policy of flexible prices and free trade on the market, the Kunming shoe factory was still bound by rigid prices set by the higher authorities of the province, and had only very few independent purchase and sale opportunities. Fixed prices were set for both the raw materials and the final products. The factories therefore made no effort to develop new models but rather manufactured shoes that required a minimal effort to produce.[16]

This lag behind the other provinces is largely due to the aversion of the then-provincial party leadership to reform. In the autumn of 1984, *Renmin ribao* (People's Daily) complained that reform efforts in Yunnan had begun relatively early but had been quickly shelved because there were too many "reservations"[17] about them. In 1981, antireform forces had already been at work to stop reform efforts with the argument that priority must be given to a "readjustment of the economy," i.e., elimination of the inequities between economic sectors. Almost all of the reform measures that had been implemented were annulled. In 1983 there were again massive attempts to restore the pre-reform structures. The intervention of the central Beijing authorities was necessary to revive the reforms,[18] at which time the provincial leadership was completely replaced.

Regions, factories, and individual producers are meant to have more rights and greater freedom of decision as a consequence of the economic reforms. Market factors are intended to compensate for the deficiencies in centralized planning. Although the freeing-up of unused capacities and the use of work incentives have resulted in an impressive economic boom throughout the country, the eventual goal of continuous growth or modernization will in the end require long-term growth strategies adapted to the conditions of each specific region.

Development strategies

After the failure of the party-mandated strategies in Yunnan, the focus has now been shifted to two different levels:

—the coordinated development of southwest China with an interregional division of labor;

—internal development that takes into account the specific characteristics of Yunnan.

Since such strategies are still in the experimental or discussion stages,[19] little can be said about the effectiveness of the model. We can, however, present and assess the most important aspects of the discussion.

Southwest China with interregional division of labor

Like the northwest, the southwest (the provinces of Guizhou, Yunnan, Sichuan, and the autonomous region of Guangxi) fears that the coastal regions will continue to receive preferential treatment, and that regional disparities in development could further grow. The Chinese scholars of the southwest have repeatedly pointed out the fact that the southwest is or could be a principal supplier of raw materials and a market for the more developed coastal regions.

Accordingly, plans are under way to develop the natural and energy resources of the region over the next 15 to 20 years. Growth strategies are being sought that can be adapted to the local conditions and economy, and the Yunnan party leadership has begun to speak of a "Yunnan way to socialism."[20]

But the region lacks the infrastructures and capital—an estimated 100 billion *yuan*—necessary to accomplish this grand plan. Since the state cannot raise such a large amount, foreign capital or capital from other provinces will need to be used. There are also plans to seek cooperative agreements for specific projects with provinces, cities, and enterprises outside of Yunnan. These projects will concentrate on the joint exploitation of natural resources, greater utilization of hydraulic power, selective development of the mountain regions, and the training of skilled workers and specialists.[21]

The Seventh Five-Year Plan (1986–1990) focused the country's economic development on the coastal region and the economically more developed parts of eastern China. Preparations for future development of the western part, such as the creation of an infrastructure and the elimination of poverty, will take up the rest of this century.[22] Therefore, a reemphasis on the southwest (and northwest) cannot take place until the early twenty-first century.

Strategies for internal development

Four regionally adapted strategies have highlighted the discussions of the future of Yunnan, three of which concentrate on the "backward" regions (mountain, minority, and western regions of the province). The fourth takes a more differentiated approach to these problem regions and may be said to be an attempt to hammer out a concept of integrated development by linking the province's more developed regions with the backward regions.[23]

Strategy 1: Priority to the mountain regions

Sixty-nine of the (in 1985) 128 counties of Yunnan are in the "mountain regions" (mountains and highlands), 33 are in mountain and valley

Table 5.7

Differences in Development in Three Mountainous Counties in Yunnan (1984) (in yuan)

County	Population	Industrial plus agricultural GOV per capita	Industrial GOV per capita	Agricultural GOV per capita	Financial income per capita	Savings per capita	Commodity turnover per capita
Zhongdian	105,861	540	154	283	30	45	183
Qiaojia	420,750	148	31	117	10	7.5	74
Bijiang	50,315	129	15	114	2.2	17	94

Source: Jingji Wenti Tansuo 1 (1985), 14.
Note: GOV = gross output value.

regions, and only 26 are entirely on the plains.

Seventy-five percent of the province's population and 60 percent of the members of ethnic minorities live in the mountain regions, which also contain most of the natural resources and 72 percent of Yunnan's tillable land. About 60 percent of grain, 50 percent of tobacco and 80 percent of tea production, 69 percent of the province's hogs, and 77 percent of its cattle are raised in these areas.[24]

Some scholars feel that these figures alone provide sufficient evidence to redirect the emphasis of development from the plains to the mountain areas. They wish to shift agriculture away from crop-raising and toward forestry and raising livestock, with a flexible diversification of the rural economy, and with an emphasis on water rice in the grain sector.[25]

There are other views, however, on the direction the development of the mountain regions should take. Some say that a sufficient grain supply must first be ensured as a precondition for a diversified economy. Although the mountain regions are not especially suited for growing grain, there is a high proportion of low-yield fields, which means that it is possible to increase grain yields considerably. If the peasants are to become prosperous, grain production must not be reduced. Another group of scholars feels that the complex structure of the mountain regions requires simultaneous development of crop-raising, forestry, and raising livestock.[26]

The contrasting of the mountain regions and the plains, as well as the attempt to develop a unified growth strategy for mountain regions, is problematic. The mountain regions alone differ vastly among themselves in structure, altitude, and climatic conditions. These dissimilar features in turn have meant differences in economic development and in the agrarian structure (see Table 5.7). This approach is therefore not suitable.

Strategy 2: Priority to minority and border regions

Seventy-six of Yunnan's counties belong to the categories of minority and border areas. They account for 49 percent of the population, 66 percent of the land area, 53 percent of the cultivated area, 67 percent of the timberland, and 74 percent of the forest area of the province (see

Table 5.8

1985 Share of Gross Output for Yunnan's Autonomous Areas as a Percentage of Yunnan Province

Year	Total GOV	Industrial GOV	Agricultural GOV	Total grain yield
1952	N.A.	40.1	N.A.	51.0
1957	46.3	35.2	53.0	50.1
1965	N.A.	30.1	N.A.	52.2
1975	N.A.	30.4	N.A.	49.9
1980	36.2	26.4	50.9	47.6
1983	35.9	26.3	48.3	47.0
1985	36.7	29.1	47.1	50.9

Source: Yunnan tongji nianjian (1986), p. 6f.
N.A.—Not available.

Table 5.8). Yet in 1985 these areas had a per capita gross output of only 429 *yuan* (Yunnan's was 849, China's as a whole was 1,580).[27]

The annual income of the minority population is in some areas far below that of the province as a whole and is often less than 30 *yuan*. Commodity exchange, division of labor, and trade are unknown to a number of minorities. Labor productivity is low: whereas the average per capita yield of grain per hectare is 274 kg at the provincial level (for China as a whole, 362 kg), in the minority regions it is only 100–200 kg. But the level of development also varies considerably within these regions. There are relatively prosperous regions, and there are very poor regions existing at the bottom of the development scale. Thus no strategy would be suitable for all minority regions alike. Even the traditional grain-growing structures are widely divergent, with rice dominating on the plains and wheat in the mountains.[28]

Strategy 3: Priority development for western Yunnan

A third strategy gives priority to the structurally more backward, western part of the province. Although it encompasses twice the land area of the eastern part, the west's gross output is not even one-third of the east's. The main reason for this is the concentration of industry in the eastern part of the province, primarily around Kunming. But grain yields and aggregate income in the west are also far below comparable figures for the east, even though the area under cultivation is greater in the west. On the other hand, the west has the largest deposits of natural resources, which could be a springboard for economic development. Before this could happen, however, infrastructures for its exploitation would have to be developed.[29] As indicated earlier, this is not likely to occur before the twenty-first century.

Strategy 4: Partition into economic zones

The advocates of this strategy argue that differences between the mountain regions and the plains, among the minority regions, and between east and west Yunnan are already quite considerable, and that a uniform strategy for these regions is therefore not practical.

Instead, they propose dividing the province into economic zones on the basis of the following primary structures:

—the different regions should base the development of their hinterlands on the central hub cities;

—technological conditions must be given due consideration in tapping resources;

—the existing and potential infrastructure must be given careful thought;

—specific industrial and agrarian structures must be taken into account; and

—the minority and border regions in particular should be promoted where appropriate.

Since in addition to Kunming there are only three other central cities (Dali, Kaiyuan, and Gejiu), Yunnan should be divided into economic zones not only that are important for the province as a whole but also that have regional importance.[30]

This strategy takes a broader view of Yunnan's complex structure. It considers the role of the cities in the development of the hinterlands, and endeavors to tie the major cities more closely into the local supply network to avoid dismantling the traditional administrative structures (e.g., the autonomous units within Yunnan). But in the current discussion on development strategies, this one has evidently not yet made much headway. Roadblocks have been thrown up not only by the so often lamented ideological conservatism of the Yunnan party leadership but also by the perceived risk that the economic gaps among the different regions could become even wider as a result of the emergence of strong, locally oriented regions turning their backs on the development of the province as a whole. Before this plan can be implemented there must first be a greater decentralization, a trained and skilled work force, and, last but not least, the necessary financial resources.

Chances of development

Yunnan's example shows that the reforms can work, especially in agriculture. But Yunnan is still not seeing the rapid growth the reforms brought elsewhere. In 1986, 4.9 million persons in Yunnan were unable to feed and cloth themselves adequately. That means that 14.4 percent of the population, the majority in the minority regions, was underprovided. This indigence can only be eliminated through the overall development of the province.[31]

Unlike the coastal provinces, Yunnan lacks a number of basic prerequisites for rapid development. The severe underdevelopment of power and transportation limits its accessibility to the outside world, and, owing to traditional structures in the province, the market integration has yet to produce noteworthy results. The requisite infrastructures must first be created and set in place if the province is profitably and effectively to develop its resource potential, market factors, private initiative, and a diversified economy.

Since the necessary capital is lacking, the only alternative is to draw on hitherto unused internal sources of financing. Specialized private plots and the new collective (township and village enterprises) and private rural factories offer good opportunities for improving the financial situations of the peasants and the counties. Still, outside help is needed if an excessive prosperity gap within China is to be avoided; such disparities are already sources of tension, and in the end imperil the total reform program.

But even if development and reform policies bear fruit, structural and technological problems will arise in Yunnan that will be difficult if not impossible to resolve within a reasonable period of time. These problems include the unfavorable production conditions in the mountain regions, the lack of sufficient tools and machinery (most farmers must still make do without farm machinery), and the scarcity of high-yield land.

If the agricultural production conditions and the tillage system do not change, agrarian yields will certainly again stagnate. The area for cultivation and sowing cannot be extended using traditional methods, and forestry and animal husbandry lack the technical prerequisites for higher productivity. If these technical problems are not solved, it will be virtually impossible—even with the reforms—to develop Yunnan's economy rapidly.

6

Population Policies: Ethnic Minorities and Migration into Minority Areas

The population problem in China

As early as the 1950s, Chinese demographers had pointed out that no successful development of the country would be possible unless the birth rate were permanently reduced: even in those days, birth control was advocated from time to time. Contraception, late marriages, clinical abortion, and voluntary sterilization were viewed as the most important methods. But with the advent of the campaigns during the "Great Leap Forward" (1958–1960), when the masses sought to change the world, a huge population was looked upon as something positive, since there would be more manpower available to build the nation. Therefore, birth control was no longer practiced.

Not until the mid-1970s did the problem of family planning return to center stage; since the late 1970s it has been systematically pursued, and the "one-child family" has been held up as the ideal. The plan calls for each couple to have only one child, and for families with one child to enjoy certain advantages (monthly subsidies, better kindergartens and schools, larger residences, larger plots of tillable land in the countryside, etc.). These advantages are to lapse if an additional child is born. However, if the first child is handicapped or dies, another birth is permissible. Exceptions to the rule are peasants in problem areas, ethnic minorities, and couples who were themselves only children, all of whom are allowed to have more than one child.

Family planning is no longer an option in China; it is a political and

Table 6.1

Projected Population Growth

	In the year 2000 (billion)	In the year 2080 (billion)
If 3 children per couple	1.414	4.260
If 2 children per couple	1.217	1.472
If 1.5 children per couple	1.125	.777
If 1 child per couple	1.054	.370

human necessity of the highest order. The 1982 population census counted slightly more than 1 billion people in China,[1] 50 percent of whom were under the age of 21. In 1987 the official natural growth rate of the population increased to 14.39 per thousand, up from 14.08 per thousand in 1986 and 11.23 per thousand in 1985.[2] If growth continues at this rate, the population will reach 1.3 billion by the end of the century, confronting China with the problem of having to provide for 100 million more people than planned. By then, an average of more than 20 million young people will reach marrying age, and about 13 million children will be born—annually. According to official statistics, feeding a child to the age of 16 costs 22,000 *yuan*, which means it will cost 220 billion *yuan* to feed 100 million people, roughly half of the fixed capital assets of all existing state enterprises in 1985.[3]

Between 1849 and 1949, China's population grew by "only" 120 million; since 1949, the population has doubled. If the 1974 growth rate had been maintained (17.5 per thousand), China's population 100 years from now would have been equivalent to the population of the entire world in 1979.[4]

Chinese social scientists have projected the Chinese population over the next 100 years based on the number of children born to each family (see Table 6.1). As currently planned, the population should grow for 68 years at an average rate of two children per couple, then for 43 years at 1.5 children per couple, and finally for 21 years at one child per couple, after which it would decline.

The following advantages are attributed to strict family planning:
—the population will see an improvement in its living standards;
—society's costs will be reduced, and it will be possible to ac-

Table 6.2

**Natural Growth Rate of Population 1949–1987
(per thousand)**

Year		Year	
1949	16.00	1968	27.38
1950	19.00	1969	26.08
1951	20.00	1970	25.83
1952	20.00	1971	23.33
1953	23.00	1972	22.16
1954	24.79	1973	20.89
1955	20.32	1974	17.48
1956	20.50	1975	15.69
1957	23.23	1976	12.66
1958	17.24	1977	12.06
1959	10.19	1978	12.00
1960	−4.57	1979	11.61
1961	3.78	1980	11.87
1962	26.99	1981	14.55
1963	33.33	1982	14.49
1964	27.64	1983	11.54
1965	28.38	1984	10.81
1966	26.22	1985	11.23
1967	25.53	1986	14.08
		1987	14.39

Source: *Zhongguo tongji nianjian* (1988), p. 90.

cumulate capital to help build the economy;

—by eliminating real and hidden unemployment, there will be a rise in labor productivity; and

—the level of education will rise, as will scientific and technical standards.[5]

Officially, the following reasons are given for the necessity of reducing the birth rate:

—China's able-bodied population is simply too large; its size approaches that of the U.S., the Soviet Union, Europe, and the other developed countries combined. The number of Chinese rural workers has increased from 200 million in the fifties to 390 million in 1987.

—The per capita cultivated acreage has decreased by one-half per rural worker compared with the fifties, when China had about 100 million ha tillable land, or 0.16 ha per capita; in 1985 the per capita

Table 6.3

Chinese Population Growth in Millions According to Census (1953–1982)

	1953 Persons	%	1964 Persons	%	1982 Persons	%
Total population	582,603	100.0	691.19	100.0	1,003,937	100.0
Han	547,283	93.9	651.30	94.2	936,704	93.0
National minorities	35,320	6.1	39.89	5.8	67,233	6.7

Source: Beijing Review 25 (1984), 24.

Table 6.4

Population Growth Rate Between Population Censuses (%)

	1964/ 1953	1982/ 1964
1. Population growth rate between two censuses		
Han	19.01	43.82
national minorities	12.95	68.57
2. Annual average growth rate between two population censuses		
Han	1.59	2.04
national minorities	1.11	2.94

Source: Beijing Review 25 (1984), 25.

tillable area was only 0.09 ha.[6] (In comparison, the 1985 figure for the U.S. is 0.953 ha, for the Soviet Union 0.9, and for India 0.27.)

—Between 1981 and 1990, openings in jobs or study vacancies need to be created annually for about 25 million school-leavers.[7]

—A population growth of over 500 million people since the fifties has created major bottlenecks in the housing sector. Just after the Communist assumption of power, there was an average of 4.5 square meters available living space per capita in the cities. By 1978 there was only 3.6 square meters.[8]

Starting in 1981, the natural population growth rate declined steadily each year until 1984, when it again began to rise (see Table 6.2). It was found that in the last few years 40 percent of all women in the countryside had given birth to three or more children although the one-child family was the declared goal of population policy. The State Statistical Bureau of the People's Republic of China confirmed that in 1986 there were 6.92 million second children and 2.88 million third children born, and in 1987 7.11 million second children and 3.79 million third children.[9] Of these, 80 percent, including third or fourth children in villages, had presumably not been approved.[10]

Economic liberties and growing migration favor the growth of the birth rate. Decreasing control mechanisms result in many births not being officially registered. The true birth rate may be, according to a random sample in 1988, about 16.2 per thousand.[11] This indicates that the official birth rates are far below the actual rates, and that the one-child policy in the countryside has failed. The goal of the population policy that the population not exceed 1.2 billion in the year 2000[12] is not attainable; 1.4 billion is a more realistic number.

Difficulties facing family planning in minority territories

Initially, ethnic minorities were by and large exempt from birth control. In 1980, however, a discussion was begun among experts of the Central Nationalities Institute, who found that since the fifties better nutrition and health care had led to higher birth rates in minority regions and a faster population growth than among the Han. Between 1964 and 1982, the proportion of the minority population increased from 5.8 percent to 6.7 percent (see Tables 6.3 and 6.4).[13]

The Institute's periodical, *Zhongguo minzu xueyuan xuebao*, looked at the case of the Yi in the autonomous prefecture of Liangshan, whose nine counties had maintained a natural growth rate of about 23 per thousand over the last few years, considerably above the country's average. It must not be thought, stated the article, that population growth in the minority regions can be disregarded simply because the ethnic groups are not large numerically; in many regions there is a high population density, and some minority regions themselves have already proposed the introduction of birth control. In fact, many places have adopted steps similar to those used in the Han regions. Thus in one Yi commune in the county of Yanbian, the propaganda emphasis is on the one-child family. The local government believes, so the article tells us, that while the minority population is numerically small, the living conditions are so arduous that birth control is appropriate. The authors are unsure whether this is the correct policy to follow. They do say that in this county there are "serious contradictions between cadres and the masses,"[14] a sign of what the local minority population thinks about all this.

Such "serious contradictions" (i.e., conflicts) must arise if birth control is forced upon the minority concerned. The desire among minorities to have many children derives from many influences, including the formerly high child mortality rate (only very few newborn survived and even today the mortality rate in minority areas is far higher than in other regions), old age care (the villages are financially unable to pay peasants a pension; children must therefore support their elderly parents), and the desire to have many sons (sons are traditionally the best guarantee of care in old age, since daughters marry into other families and leave the family). Birth control seems to many minorities to be an attempt at assimilation, making family planning in these regions an explosive issue.

In the early eighties there were three views on how birth control should be dealt with in the minority regions: (1) implement birth control, reducing natural growth to less than zero per thousand until the end of the century (as in the case of the Han); (2) do not introduce birth control, because minority regions are large in area, but sparsely populated; (3) develop planned population growth in these regions.[15]

An article in the journal *Renkou yanjiu* (Population Studies) advocated birth control in regions where the level of production was low but the population was large. In the autonomous prefecture Linxia of the Hui (Gansu province), population growth was over 40 per thousand per year. From 1973 on, the prefecture was no longer self-sufficient in grain, and was forced to rely on state subsidies of up to almost 74,000 tons yearly. Bottlenecks occurred in education, even though the number of primary schools increased from 175 in the early fifties to 1,472 in the late seventies, the number of secondary schools from 3 to 44, and the number of teachers from 178 to 8,521. In 1978 there were no places in primary schools for 32 percent of school-age children, nor were there any vacancies in the lower levels of secondary schools for 10 percent of those coming from primary school, nor in the upper level of secondary schools for 60 percent of lower-level graduates. There were too many pupils, and there was no money for additional teachers, premises, or school buildings.

Bottlenecks also occurred in employment. In 1978 there were 6,639 people leaving school and waiting for a job assignment; thereafter the number increased by 8,000 yearly, although there were only 2,400 jobs per year available. In housing, transportation, kindergartens, hospitals, cultural institutions, supplies, etc., similar constrictions occurred. All this despite the fact that this prefecture had been practicing birth control since 1973, and the population growth decreased from 28.7 per thousand in 1973 to 14.7 per thousand in 1978.

In the same article, the authors proposed that in the sparsely settled minority regions with sufficient tillable farmland, the birth of children should be encouraged. For example, in 1981 the autonomous county of Aksay of the Kazaks (Gansu province) had pastureland with rich natural resources but only 7,000 inhabitants (2,600 Kazak), indicating a relatively strong economic potential. However, the climate is harsh and cold, and health care is rudimentary. The birth rate is low, and the population grew by an average of only 1.5 per thousand annually to 1981, increasing by only 320 persons between 1950 and 1980. Health care as well as protection for mothers and children should be improved in such regions and measures should be taken to encourage a strong birth rate.

The authors also recommended that the Han should be treated no differently in minority regions than in Han regions, retaining the one-child family rule; as for members of ethnic minorities, population policy should be decided according to the local conditions and according to the specific situation.[16]

An official of the family planning office of Tianshui prefecture (Gansu province) advocated controlling population growth in minority regions, alleging that the population growth rate was too high in these regions and that in fact they had a higher growth rate than the Han. In the Ningxia Autonomous Region of the Hui, the population has tripled since 1980, while the population of the Xinjiang Autonomous Region of the Uygur increased by 78.2 percent between 1949 and 1978. Therefore, control of population growth in densely inhabited minority regions is necessary in the interests of the country as a whole, although in thinly inhabited regions it is not.[17]

Other scholars warned against proceeding too schematically in population policy for minorities. Birth control should be applied in the cities as well as the regions, since a too rapid growth among minorities in the urban population will aggravate the already existing problems in supplies, schooling, housing, and jobs. Yet even in the cities the policy toward the minorities must be more flexible than toward the Han.[18]

In the end, the view prevailed that population growth must be curbed in densely inhabited minority regions, but that small minorities should be subject to more elastic and liberal birth control regulations in their regions than in the Han regions[19]—i.e., that the number of children per family may be higher for minorities. Thus in the Liangshan Autonomous Prefecture of the Yi (Sichuan province), it was decided in 1981 that urban Han should have only one child, but that the Yi could have two and Yi peasants even three. As for economic sanctions (for Han everywhere who have more than two children) the procedures for members of national minorities should be less rigid and take into consideration the "feelings" of the minorities.

Although coercive measures are officially prohibited, the pressure on local officials to report successes in birth planning is so great that strong measures are regularly resorted to. There are allegations from minority regions that birth planning was forcibly introduced. Members of minorities, it is stated, are terrified every time they hear the word family planning. A local official need only approach their houses and they and their children go into hiding.[20] In the Gansu district of Zhugqu, the birth rate was reduced from 12.9 per thousand in 1978 to 10.7 per thousand in 1979 through compulsory sterilization and compulsory abortion. Strong-arm tactics and medical bungling also produced serious tensions and resentment between Han officials and the Tibetans.[21]

Current practice

In 1982 the central authorities in Beijing decided that the minorities should also be involved in family planning, and gave the autonomous administration units the right to develop their own family-planning policies.[22] In 1984 the central authorities ruled that the one-child family should be encouraged for minorities comprising more than 10 million members (which has so far affected only one group, the Zhuang) and that all other nationalities could have two children per couple, and under special circumstances even three; four children or more were not to be permitted.[23]

The margin of discretion allowed the autonomous units by the central authorities has resulted in widely varying regulations. The party committee in the Xinjiang Autonomous Region stipulated in October 1985 that minority married couples living in cities could have two children, and those living in the countryside could have three and in exceptional cases four. The one-child family was not promulgated among these people.[24] In the sparsely populated Tibet Autonomous Region, urban Tibetans were allowed two children and in exceptional cases three. No restrictions were set for Tibet's rural regions;[25] quite apart from the impossibility of monitoring the observance of these restrictions, they could have been implemented only through the use of violence.

The regulations in Liangshan Autonomous Prefecture (for the Yi two children in the cities and three in the countryside) have already been mentioned.[26] In the Hulun Buir League* of Inner Mongolia Autonomous Region, the government stipulated that there would be no restrictions on the number of children for the Daur, Ewenki, Oroqen, and Hezhen, but that there must be three years between each child. Mongolians, Hui, Manchu, Koreans, and the descendants of Russians with Chinese citizenship may have two children, and Mongolian shepherds on the pasturelands may have three.[27]

The regulations are especially strict in Qinghai, which has a minority population of 38.9 percent. There, people working for the state (whether they be Han or members of national minorities) may have only one child. The one-child family is also encouraged in the countryside; households with shortages of family laborers (so-called "problem households") may have two children by special "permission," but not three. However, the autonomous units of this province may set special regulations,[28] and most of the autonomous prefectures in that province have set other quotas.

In Haibei Autonomous Prefecture of the Tibetans (Qinghai province), the one-child family has been stipulated for all, but in general (i.e., "with permission") peasants may have two children and shepherds three, although the children must be spaced by at least four

---

*A league in Inner Mongolia is the equivalent of a prefecture.

years.[29] In truth, if family-planning policy were too rigid, the nomadic shepherds of this area would merely migrate into other provinces or autonomous regions having less rigorous regulations.

In practice, minorities in remote areas are quite casual in their observance of official regulations. Even in the cities, where the authorities have greater means of social control, the minority birth rate is declining only slowly. In 1983, in Ürümqi, the capital of Xinjiang Autonomous Region, 94.5 percent of the Han but only 36.3 percent of the Moslem Hui adhered to the family planning policy; 42.4 percent of the Kazak and 36.2 percent of the Uygur in the city had more than three children in the last few years, and 14.7 percent of the Uygur had even more than five.[30] In 1986, according to official data, 99.7 percent of the Han but only 66 percent of minorities adhered to family planning policies.[31]

One source of the problem in Xinjiang is that faithful Moslems, constitute a large portion of the population, regard many children as a "blessing of Allah" and reject family planning on religious grounds.[32] The Chinese leadership therefore was forced to enjoin the Moslem religious leaders to proclaim publicly that family planning does not go against the Koran and that in fact it is also practiced in Pakistan, in Malaysia, and Indonesia.[33]

Problems of population planning
in minority regions

The number of children per family in minorities is almost universally higher than in Han (see Table 6.5). For example, while the Han population in Sichuan increased by 45 percent between 1964 and 1982, that of the minorities went up by 110 percent, increasing their proportion of the population from 2.6 percent in 1964 to 3.7 percent in 1982. The much higher mortality rate of minorities is offset by the birth rate, and the population's growth rates in the autonomous prefectures are much higher than in the province (see Table 6.6).[34]

The multinationality province of Guizhou in the southwest shows a similar trend. The proportion of minorities increased by 85 percent between 1964 and 1982 (3.8 percent growth rate annually), while the Han population grew by only 60.9 percent (2.7 percent annual growth rate).[35] Here again, both birth rates and even rates for births into

Table 6.5

Number of Children per Family in Sichuan Province in 1981 (in percent of all births)

Region	1	2	3	4 or more
Sichuan province as a whole	56.4	24.1	9.5	10.0
Garze Tibetan Autonomous Prefecture	25.8	18.3	15.2	40.7
Aba Tibetan Autonomous Prefecture	22.8	17.4	15.2	44.6
Liangshan Yi Autonomous Prefecture	24.4	17.8	13.6	44.2

Source: *Zhongguo shaoshu minzu* 12 (1985), 103.

Table 6.6

Population Rates in Sichuan Province in 1981 (per thousand)

Region	Birth rate	Death rate	Natural growth rate
Sichuan province	17.96	7.02	10.94
Aba Tibetan Autonomous Prefecture	27.85	9.61	18.24
of which Zoige county[a]	33.95	12.37	21.58
Garze Tibetan Autonomous Prefecture	29.93	12.11	17.82
of which Dege county[b]	33.21	10.94	22.27
Liangshan Yi Autonomous Prefecture	32.71	11.34	21.37
of which Zhaojue county[c]	47.93	21.26	26.67

Source: *Zhongguo shaoshu minzu* 12 (1985), 101.

Notes: [a] 81% Tibetan population.
[b] 96% Tibetan population.
[c] 93% Yi population.

families already having children are far above the national average (see Table 6.7). Unfortunately, economic growth, the education and health systems, jobs, urban services, and housing in the minority regions have not kept pace with the population growth, and bottlenecks have accordingly occurred.[36]

But fears are regularly voiced that the minorities could over the long term become a majority. The somewhat exaggeratedly rigorous family-planning policy seems, in part, to be rooted in this anxiety. A

Table 6.7

Birth Rates in Guizhou 1981 (per thousand)

	Births	
	per 1000	in families w/children (%)
China	20.91	27.15
Guizhou province of which:	27.89	55.93
Han	25.83	54.03
Dong	25.97	49.04
Yi	28.74	61.46
Bouyei	30.62	55.63
Gelo	31.31	76.19
Miao	32.00	61.47
Shui	35.15	62.34

Source: *Guizhou shehui kexue* 5 (1987), 21.

Table 6.8

Projected Growth of Minority Population (in millions)

Year	If previous growth (20 per thousand)	If 4 children per married couple	If 3 children per married couple
1990	70.0	79.2	72.5
2000	85.3	99.5	86.0
2010	104.0	131.0	110.0
2030	154.6	221.0	141.0
2050	229.7	378.0	193.0
2080	416.0	864.0	297.0

Source: Tian Xueyuan, *Xin shiqi renkou lun* (1983), p. 147.

population expert calculated that the Han could be only a bare majority, if at all, in just 100 years if the one-child family were to become the rule for the Han (for projected growth of the minority population, see Table 6.8); thus there would be ''only'' 370 million people living in China by the year 2080, at which point the minorities would have become a ma-

Table 6.9

Average Age of Ethnic Minorities with a Population of over 1 Million (1981)

Nationality	Average age
Minorities as a whole	19.41
of which:	
Korean	24.32
Manchu	21.28
Hui	20.38
Tibetan	19.72
Tujia	19.66
Uygur	19.61
Zhuang	19.46
Dong	19.35
Bouyei	19.33
Bai	19.26
Mongolian	19.08
Yao	18.81
Yi	18.25
Miao	18.21
Hani	18.03

Source: *Beijing Review* 25 (1984), 28.

Table 6.10

Comparison of China's Age Groups with International Standards (% of population)

Region	0–14 years	15–64 years	Over 65 years
Average for all countries	35	59	6
Developed countries	23	66	11
Developing countries	39	57	4
China	34	62	5
of which ethnic minorities	39	56	5

Source: *Beijing Review* 25 (1984), 28.

jority. But this is probably unrealistic both for the Han and for the minorities since, after a period of restriction, the number of children should increase among the Han as well. Moreover, the one-child family

Table 6.11

Number of Births to Women Between the Ages of 15 and 64 (1982)

Number of children	Live births (%)		Surviving children (%)	
	National minorities	Han	National minorities	Han
0	32.1	32.2	33.1	32.7
1	9.1	11.1	10.8	12.2
2	10.0	12.3	12.4	14.1
3	9.9	11.3	12.8	13.4
4	9.5	9.7	11.6	11.2
5	8.3	7.7	8.8	8.0
6	6.9	6.0	5.6	4.8
7	5.1	4.0	2.9	2.3
8	3.8	2.7	1.3	0.9
9	2.3	1.4	0.5	0.3
10	1.5	0.9	0.1	0.1
11	0.7	0.3		
12	0.4	0.2		
13	0.2	0.1		
More than 14	0.2	0.1	.06	.02
Total	100.0	100.0	100.0	100.0

Source: *Zhongguo 1982 nian renkou pucha* (1985), p. 482ff.

Table 6.12

Comparison of Birth Rates of Han and Ethnic Minorities (1982)

	Live births (%)		Surviving children (%)	
	National minorities	Han	National minorities	Han
Family size				
More than 5 children	21.0	15.7	10.5	8.4
More than 10 children	1.5	0.7	0.06	0.02
Fewer than 3 children	51.2	55.6	56.3	59.0

Source: See Table 6.11.

can hardly be imposed on rural regions of China. Finally, a large segment of the minorities will have been assimilated over the next 100 years—as they were at the beginning of this century—and will be indistinguishable from the Han.

Table 6.13

Women of Child-bearing Age without Children (%)

Nationality	No births or no surviving children
Han	32.7
Total minorities	33.1
of which:	
Achang	36.7
Dulong	38.3
Daur	39.0
Lhoba	38.9
Uzbek	40.7
Tatar	41.5
Oroqen	43.1
Xibe	42.2
Hezhen	46.6
Ewenki	46.1
Moinba	70.0

Sources: *Zhongguo 1982 nian renkou pucha* (1985), p. 482ff.

Similar fears are also voiced in the autonomous regions and multinationality provinces. It is said in Xinjiang that if the minorities continue to have an average of 2.5 children in the cities and 3.5 children in the countryside, there could be 11.3 million minority members in Xinjiang in the year 2000 but only 6.6 million Han.[37] This calculation, however, does not take into account the number of migrants from Han areas who arrive in Xinjiang every day.

Despite these points, there is much to indicate that the minority population will continue to grow more rapidly than the Han population. In fact, the population census of 1981 classified 51.4 percent of the minority population (as compared to 46.1 percent of the Han) as under the age of 20 (see Tables 6.9 and 6.10). Birth rates and natural growth rates for the national minorities should therefore continue to rise. Although the number of live births is lower and infant mortality is higher than among the Han, the minorities have more births and more children per family (see Tables 6.11 and 6.12).

The birth rates in the autonomous regions and in provinces with a large proportion of ethnic minorities are higher than those in other areas. The highest rates in 1987 were found in (*Zhongguo tongji nianjian*, 1988, p. 99):

	Birth rate per thousand
China as a whole	21.0
Auton. region of Xinjiang	27.3
Auton. region of Ningxia	25.1
Auton. region of Guangxi	24.4
Yunnan	24.0
Guizhou	23.7
Hunan	23.6
Shandong	23.4
Qinghai	22.6

However, the minority areas have the highest mortality rates (*Zhongguo tongji nianjian*, 1988, p. 99):

	Deaths per thousand
China	6.7
Auton. region of Xinjian	8.7
Guizhou	8.5
Yunnan	8.4
Tibet	7.8

The minority areas also lead in the rate of births beyond one child. The highest percentage of such births in 1988 excluding Tibet, where no data is available, were found in (*Jingji cankao*, Dec. 24, 1988):

	%
Auton. region of Xinjiang	45.2
Hainan	32.0
Auton. region of Guangxi	30.2
Guizhou	30.1
Auton. region of Ningxia	29.9
Qinghai	28.3
Yunnan	23.7

In relatively well-developed provinces and cities, this rate is very low, for instance (*Jingji cankao*, Dec. 24, 1988):

	%
Shanghai	0.0
Liaoning	1.4
Beijing	1.9
Zhejiang	3.6
Tianjiu	3.8
Jilin	4.0

Table 6.14

Population Development of Oroqen in the Great Xing'anling Mountains (1980–1982)

Year	Births	Total	Deaths Due to natural causes	Deaths Due to unnatural causes
1980	5	20	11	9
1981	7	13	6	7
1982	3	13	5	8
Total	15	46	22	24

Source: Zhongguo shehui kexue (1986), 84.

The dilemma of the small minorities

The breakdown of the data in Table 6.13 by nationality shows that about the same proportion of Han and minority women of child-bearing age still have no children. For smaller minorities, however, the situation is much different. Although minorities tend to marry much earlier than the legal age (22 years for men and 20 years for women),[38] a growing number of women from small minorities of child-bearing age have no children.

Because of this phenomenon and other factors, smaller minorities are likely to become extinct or to be assimilated in the not-too-distant future. The hunting peoples of northeastern China are the most threatened. Infectious diseases and alcoholism have been decimating these groups since the end of the last century, and the situation has not improved much since the Communist assumption of power, although the population figures have again improved slightly (see for example those for the Oroqen in Table 6.14). The destruction of the economic and social structures of these peoples and cultural shock are surely attributable to these problems, which can be observed worldwide among smaller ethnic groups.

The number of deaths in small minorities far exceeds the number of births, and the number of "unnatural deaths" is over 50 percent. In 1965, 186 Ewenki, who were nomadic hunters in Ergun Zuoqi (Inner Mongolia), were made sedentary. Since then, five Ewenki have been

Table 6.15

Proportion of Persons over the Age of 60 by Nationality (1982)

Nationality	%	Nationality	%
Han	15.9	Jinuo	6.7
Russian	11.5	Shui	6.6
She	8.8	Bulang	6.5
Naxi	8.0	Jingpo	6.5
Uygur	7.9	Hui	6.4
Bouyei	7.7	Lisu	6.3
Tajik	7.7	Miao	6.3
Tibetan	7.6	Yi	6.2
Tujia	7.5	Qiang	6.2
Jing	7.4	Li	6.2
Achang	7.4	Xibe	6.1
Dulong	7.2	Uzbek	6.0
Mulam	7.2	Bonan	5.9
Bai	7.2	Lahu	5.8
Lhoba	7.1	Hani	5.7
Moinba	7.1	Daur	5.6
Manchu	7.1	Dongxiang	5.5
Tujia	7.1	Mongolian	5.4
Pumi	7.0	Va	5.3
Nu	7.0	Tatar	5.3
Dai	6.9	Gaoshan	5.2
Kirgiz	6.9	Salar	5.1
Maonan	6.9	Tu	4.9
Gelo	6.8	Yugur	4.7
Dong	6.8	Kazak	4.6
Korean	6.8	Hezhen	4.0
Yao	6.8	Ewenki	3.7
Deang	6.8	Oroqen	2.5

Source: *Zhongguo renmin gongheguo laonian renkou dituji* (1986), p. 10/3.

murdered by tribe members who were drunk, two have committed suicide after consuming alcohol, and 13 infants died shortly after birth from alcohol intoxication. In addition, eight Ewenki have been given prison sentences for alcohol-related manslaughter.[39]

An article in *Beijing Review* on "birth protection" for the Ewenki, Daur, and Oroqen in Inner Mongolia helps explain this phenomenon. The following measures have been adopted for these ethnic groups:

—"improvement" in living conditions through the abandonment of a nomadic life;

—free medical care;
—prohibition of marriages among relatives, and encouragement of marriages between members of different nationalities;
—prohibition of alcohol;
—the use of scientific methods of birth control.[40]

Many vital social structures were altered and denied these groups. Measures such as forced settlement and "prohibition of marriages among relatives" are grave attacks on the cultures and customs of these people, and are destroying their cultural and social fabric. Alcoholism and deracination are the results of measures that were undoubtedly well-intentioned. Once torn from their traditional culture and mode of livelihood, and forbidden their habits and customs, such peoples are doomed to extinction, especially when they are numerically as small as these Tungusic groups. These people are quickly assimilated through "encouragement of marriages between members of different nationalities." Settling the remainder in villages with predominantly Han populations and encouraging mixed marriages accelerate this process. The periodical *Zhongguo shehui kexue* (Social Science in China) reports, not without some pride, that the number of Oroqen and Ewenki would rise again as a consequence of mixed marriages, whose offspring are granted the status of minority members.[41] But are the offspring really still Ewenki and Oroqen? Children from mixed marriages receive a Han upbringing, no longer speak any language other than Han Chinese, and as a rule also consider themselves Han. They are members of "national minorities" only on paper.

The life expectancy of ethnic minorities

The life expectancy of minorities is lower than that of Han. There are manifold reasons for this, among them poorer living, work, geographical, and nutritional conditions. Far fewer minority members live past the age of 60 (see Table 6.15). In northwest China, in the autonomous regions of Ningxia, Inner Mongolia, and Xinjiang, and in the multinationality provinces of Qinghai and Gansu, the over-sixty population makes up less than 6 percent of the total population, and in Xinjiang it decreased from 6.8 percent in 1952 to 5.8 percent in 1982.[42]

The physical constitution of minorities is also claimed to have deteriorated, allegedly due to early marriages and births. However, these are not new, but in fact very old, customs. Why should a people's collective health suddenly deteriorate because of this? Might it be that physical constitution is an excuse to intervene into the social structure of minorities?[43] A growing susceptibility to disease and serious environmental pollution, which are mentioned only in passing, would seem to be more important factors here.[44]

Migration into minority regions

The ratio of Han in Inner Mongolia relative to Mongolians increased between 1958 and 1968 from 6:1 to 12:1.[45] In Xinjiang, the Han population increased from 6.2 percent in 1953 to almost 40 percent of the total in 1973.[46] The main reason for this has been migration into these regions. Between 1953 and 1970, an estimated 12.25 million Han migrated to the northwest from other parts of the country,[47] with the same trend occurring in other minority regions.[48] Tibet was the least affected by migrations owing to its geographical location, which is unattractive to the Han.

Migration has been mainly the result of resettling Han from the crowded centers of Eastern China, restationing of army units, dispatching those leaving secondary school from the cities into these regions, and unofficial immigration.[49] Four migration periods may be distinguished:

1. 1954–1960: In 1954, 22 million, in 1955, 25 million, and in 1956, 30 million persons migrated to other parts of the country. A peak of 33 million persons was reached in 1960. These were workers and their families who were sent into virgin regions, or peasants who were systematically resettled from the densely populated regions of eastern China (Shandong, Jiangsu, Zhejiang) to the northeast (Heilongjiang) or northwest (Ningxia, Xinjiang) to cultivate new land.

2. 1961–1965: 19 million, 13 million, and 15 million persons resettled in 1961, 1963, and 1965, respectively.

3. 1966–1976: in 1966, 14 million, between 1967 and 1969, 5–6 million, and between 1970 and 1976, 11–16 million persons migrated. Six million persons—one-third of its population—emigrated into Inner Mongolia alone during this period (there are no data available on how much of this was due to the policies of the Cultural Revolution).

4. 1977–1984: 14–23 million persons migrated from one part of the

Table 6.16

Minority and Han Populations in Inner Mongolia and Xinjiang (1947–1976)

Region	Total population (in millions)	Minorities Population (in millions)	% of total	Han Population (in millions)	% of total
Inner Mongolia					
1947	N.A.	N.A.	25.0	N.A.	75.0
1958	8.2	1.2	14.6	7.0	85.4
1959	9.7	1.3	13.4	8.4	86.6
1969	13.0	1.0	7.7	12.0	92.3
1976	8.6	0.4	4.7	8.2	95.3
Xinjiang					
1949	3.7	3.4	91.9	0.3	8.1
1953	4.9	4.6	93.9	0.3	6.1
1957	5.6	4.3	76.8	1.3	23.2
1960	7.0	5.0	71.4	2.0	28.6
1975	10.0	6.2	62.0	3.8	38.0

Source: Scharping, *Umsiedlungsprogramme für Chinas Jugend 1955–1980* (1981), p. 436.
N.A.—Information not available.

country to another.[50]

Most of the migrants moved without official permission. Two-thirds of the migrants in Heilongjiang and 60 percent of those in Xinjiang immigrated "blind" (*mangmu*), i.e., on their own initiative. During the great famine of 1959–61 in particular, hordes came from the famine areas to Xinjiang, which at that time was not affected.[51]

The population growth due to migration was greatest in the north—Inner Mongolia, Xinjiang, Ningxia, Qinghai, and Heilongjiang. Whereas the overall population of the country increased by 50 percent between 1952 and 1982, it doubled in some of these regions (see examples in Table 6.16). About 25–30 million persons migrated to other parts of the country between 1949 and 1984, 15 million of these into the above mentioned provinces and autonomous regions. Of these 15 million, 23 percent migrated to Heilongjiang, 34 percent to Xinjiang, 30 percent to Inner Mongolia, 29 percent to Qinghai, and 23 percent to Ningxia.[52] (These migratory patterns are shown in Map 6.1.)

Map 6.1. **Chinese Internal Migrations.**

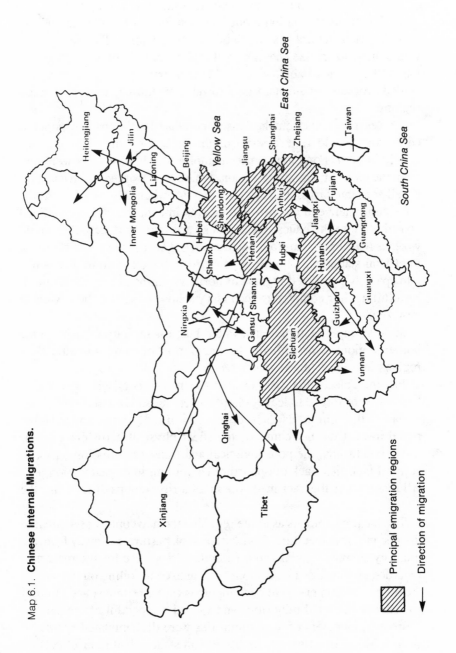

East China Sea

South China Sea

Yellow Sea

Heilongjiang

Jilin

Liaoning

Beijing

Inner Mongolia

Shandong

Jiangsu

Shanghai

Zhejiang

Taiwan

Hebei

Anhui

Fujian

Shanxi

Henan

Hubei

Jiangxi

Guangdong

Ningxia

Gansu Shaanxi

Hunan

Guangxi

Guizhou

Sichuan

Yunnan

Xinjiang

Qinghai

Tibet

Principal emigration regions

Direction of migration

The official reasons for this internal migration policy were:

1. The local population alone was insufficient to open up and exploit the rich natural resources of northern China. The newcomers would help to utilize the raw material resources of these regions, make the land tillable, and build industry. Han specialists and skilled workers would help also to develop the economies of these regions.

2. Resettlements from the densely populated to the sparsely populated regions would relieve some of the burden on the former to the benefit of both. For a long time, unemployed school-leavers were sent from the cities into minority regions where they worked in agriculture, usually on state farms, thereby relieving the urban labor market. At the same time their education would, it was intended, make a beneficial contribution to the educationally backward regions (where they could work as teachers, "barefoot doctors," bookkeepers, etc.). According to official statistics, 12 million youth from the cities were dispatched into sparsely populated regions of northern China during the Cultural Revolution after completing secondary school as part of the "Xiafang movement."

3. A stronger Han presence would buttress military security in the border regions and facilitate the integration of minorities and their regions into the Chinese mainstream.

Innumerable difficulties awaited the newcomers who grudgingly left—or were forced to leave—their homes: harsh climatic conditions, diseases, the minorities themselves (who usually were not well-disposed toward the newcomers), the sheer physical hardships of poor living conditions, the poor logistical and transport situations, lack of cultural facilities, lack of opportunities for continuing education, etc. All these things together made life in minority regions difficult for the Han.

The local inhabitants as a rule regarded the newcomers as a threat to their economy and culture. Han settlers took pastureland away from the minority shepherds, and youth from the cities were for the most part regarded as "useless mouths to feed," unused to toiling on the land.[53] Often the newcomers were contemptuous of the religious and cultural customs of the local minorities and were disrespectful of the people. Moreover, members of local minorities were discriminated against in factory hiring practices. All these circumstances had their effects on the relations between the Han immigrants and the local minorities.

Because of the ill will felt by many minorities toward the Han immigrants, the Han found themselves corralled into state farms in order to separate them from the minorities. Relations between Han employees on the state farms and the local minorities were often envenomed and fraught with hate, and serious clashes occurred, especially during the Cultural Revolution. A catalog of prohibitions for Han working on state farms in minority regions in the Xishuangbanna Autonomous Prefecture shows what these clashes were all about: the Han lack of respect for the customs and way of life of the local minorities, confiscation of their land, destruction of property, environmental pollution, deforestation, slaughtering of the minorities' livestock by the state farms, etc.[54] For this reason, minority representatives are today demanding that such immigrations be stopped and (as in Tibet) that the Han leave these regions (excepting persons with certain needed skills).

The immigrants were a heavy burden on the regions in many respects. The northwest, primarily a livestock region, suffered considerably at the hands of the migrants, who attempted to convert pastures into tillable fields. Pastureland retreated, the desert advanced, and the ecological balance was seriously disrupted.[55] In Qinghai, the per capita grain yield decreased from 290 kg in 1952 to 284 kg in 1979 and 247 kg in 1985. Livestock diminished from 7.07 million head in 1980 to 5.89 million head in 1985.[56] Xinjiang, with 400 kg grain per capita in 1966, had been a grain exporter to other provinces (175 thousand tons); in 1980 it was producing only 301 kg per capita and 100,000 tons had to be imported.[57] The population of central Gansu doubled since 1949, but grain production increased by only 60 percent.[58]

Perspective on long-term effects of Han migration

Immigration policy was and is a violation of the rights of the autonomy of minorities, even if it has helped to create an industrial base for their regions. The autonomous administrative units have neither the means nor the right to undertake countermeasures. The influx of large segments of the Han population undermines the strength of the autonomous minority of a region, and it can also disrupt the economic structure (e.g., by the influx of peasants into pasturelands and forest regions) and result in the cultural dominance of the Han. Thus, in addition to being politically preeminent, the Han can easily secure for themselves leading positions in economic development and undermine the development and identity of the local minority population. Tensions between nationalities, as in Xinjiang, Inner Mongolia,[59] Tibet, and other regions, are the natural consequence of this immigration policy, which cannot be justified only in terms of providing these regions with a needed skilled workforce. If that were the case, it would be sufficient to send skilled workers to minority regions for a specified period of time to train the local workforce. A more plausible explanation for the immigration policy is that the over-population in the densely populated regions must be reduced, and the rich and manifold natural resources of the autonomous regions must be put to use. In addition, the Chinese leadership is not certain of the loyalty of the minorities and feels that the implantation of a Han majority in minority regions would offer a natural border defense as well as protection against any future Soviet-supported appeal to, say, Uygur national sentiment.[60]

Assimilation is not directly intended (as it was during the Cultural Revolution), but the creation of a Han majority in the minority regions will undoubtedly encourage it. And the fact that the minorities perceive it in this way is shown by their resistance to the influx of Han and to mixed marriages.

Autonomy, if it is to work, cannot be merely a theoretical directive to preserve the "purity" of the minority regions. If autonomy is to have a meaning, the minorities, who for centuries have been pushed aside by the Han and subjected to the pressure to assimilate, must be permitted to decide themselves on any influx (or departure) of Han cadres—who usually have no desire to remain in the autonomous regions. For example, many Han youth streamed back to the cities from the minority regions following the 1977 thaw, and delegations came to Beijing where they publicized their catastrophic living conditions on big character posters. In November 1980, thousands of youth (mainly from Shanghai) demonstrated in Aksu (Xinjiang) for the right to return to their homes.

If the minorities have no freedom to decide on these matters, then they also have no genuine autonomy. It will be possible for the minorities to identify with Chinese state policy only if they have a minority and autonomy policy that safeguards the interests of the minorities and grants them broad powers of self-administration and decision-making. An influx of Han predicated solely on the fear of the Chinese leadership that the minorities might place themselves on the side of an adversary in case of conflict, or that under certain circumstances (as in Tibet) they might break away from China, is not a viable way to approach or solve the problem. The minority fear of assimilation will only grow, and conflicts between Han and the minorities will be a foregone conclusion.

Concrete proposals of extensive resettlement of Han in the sparsely populated regions already exist as part of a general population policy. The uneven distribution of the population, it is argued, makes such steps necessary. From the Han standpoint this is quite understandable. In 1985, 96 percent of the population lived in eastern China, which covers less than half of the country's area (see Table 6.17), and only 4 percent lived in western China.

Since the area available for cultivation is much smaller in the east than in the west, it is argued that there is a tremendous potential in the west for creating tillable acreage, whereas in the east a decline in farmed acreage is to be expected due to the growth of cities. The encouragement of natural population growth in the west and a restriction on births in the east must be complemented by the development and implementation of resettlement projects from east to west. This would help to achieve a more balanced distribution of the population and productive forces, and facilitate the tapping and exploitation of raw materials and the economic development of the minorities of these regions. An increase in the population density in the western border regions from six persons per square km to 20 would mean that 70 million persons could be resettled.[61]

But opinions on this proposal are widely varying. The sociologist Fei Xiaotong thinks that primary reliance must be placed on the local population in developing the minority regions, with skilled labor being imported from without. Blind migration must be curbed, and replaced by planned migration.[62] Fei speaks of resettling 60 million people within three decades.[63]

While some scholars advocate large scale resettlements to the north-west,[64] others warn of the consequences for logistics and ecology. The area under cultivation is slight, and the self-sufficiency of these regions with grain is not assured.[65] Economic development has

Table 6.17

China's Population Distribution (1985)

Region	Population Number in millions	%	Surface area in millions of km²	%	Population density (per km²)
Eastern zone	1,001.09	96	4.6	48	207
Western zone[a]	44.23	4	5.0	52	6

Source: Zhongguo tongji nianjian (1986), p. 93f.
Note: [a]The Western zone includes Xinjiang, Gansu, Qinghai, Ningxia, and Tibet.

Table 6.18

Minority Population in Autonomous Regions

Autonomous region	Total minority population (%) 1982	1985	1987
Guangxi	38.3	39.0	39.1
Inner Mongolia	15.6	16.4	17.5
Ningxia	31.9	32.5	32.9
Tibet	95.1	96.4	95.4
Xinjiang	59.6	60.7	61.4

Source: Zhongguo 1982 nian renkou pucha (1985), p. 218f; Zhongguo tongji nianjian (1986), p. 7, and (1988) p. 84.

not, it is argued, kept pace with population growth.[66]

Chinese scholars have yet to question the fact that the minorities have in some cases become numerical minorities in their own regions because of Han migration. The influx has declined somewhat due to the change in nationality policy in the early eighties; also, the minorities are beginning to catch up because of their higher birth rates (see Table 6.18).

Important raw materials are situated in minority regions, and China's economic development is impossible without opening them up. But these regions are also border regions and sparsely populated, while the east is over populated. It is not surprising, therefore, that large, ambitious resettlement projects are a topic of discussion. These projects will be difficult to implement without provoking resistance from the minorities concerned. Respect of minority autonomy goes against the interests of population policy and certainly against the interests of development of the country as a whole. How this problem is dealt with will be of crucial importance for future minority policy and for the relationship between the ethnic minorities and the Han.

7

Religion, Religious Policy, and Ethnic Minorities

Many ethnic minorities in China profess religions other than those of the Han. In the northwest, Islam is a major influence among the Hui and Uygur, which are the second and third largest nationalities.[1] Lamaism is the religion of the Tibetans and Mongolians as well as of a number of smaller ethnic groups. In the south, Mahayana-Buddhism has a foothold. Animism, animatism, and Shamanism still exist among numerous minor peoples.[2] This intertwining of religion and nationality makes the religious question a touchy one.

What is "religion" in China?

Because religion in China is not the same as religion in the West, present-day Chinese religious policy cannot be explained by either theological or Marxist standards, or be measured by Western concepts alone. An antireligious attitude has a long tradition in China, dating from the fourth century B.C., when many of the learned equated religion with superstition.

The question of the meaning of life, which has motivated European philosophers for centuries, has never been a major concern in China. Nor was life after death a subject of consideration for Confucian and Taoist scholars. When asked about the essence of death, Confucius replied, "If we do not even know what life is, how can we know anything about death." There was no word in Chinese for religion in the Western sense. Traditionally, the terms "doctrine" (*jiao*) or, more precisely, the "doctrine of ancestors" (*zong*) were the terms used, and no fundamental distinction was drawn between religion and doctrine either theoretically or linguistically. For the Chinese, a religion is one doctrine among many others. Religion does not rule out other doctrines and cannot lay claim to a prior right of being the one and only infallible opinion or school of thought. The multitude of doctrines in China have never needed clearly defined demarcation among them, as have religions in the Western concept.

There are three main intellectual traditions that have left their marks on China: Confucianism, Taoism, and Buddhism. The first two are China's own offspring, and both existed for about 500 years before Buddhism gained a foothold in China. But even before Confucianism and Taoism, other religious and cosmological ideas such as animism (worship of natural deities, fertility rites, and cults, and especially the worship of ancestors) existed for 1,000 years; it is out of these that the two developed, each in its own way.

These three traditions have influenced one another and changed considerably over the course of time, but they have never merged. The upper strata of officials and scholars have almost universally adhered to the philosophical world-view of Confucianism; the common people, however, did not regard themselves as part of only one of the intellectual traditions, but instead visited the temples of all those religions. Confucianism, Taoism, and Buddhism in their religious forms were combined in the so-called "folk religion."[3] In China, the term "*san wei yi*" is used to mean that three (religions) are only one.

The positive Confucian view of the world and the negative Taoist view complement one another. It has been said that Chinese are Confucians when fortune is kind to them, Taoists when things are going badly, and Buddhists when death approaches. A person who fails may retreat disappointed, and regard things from the outside in the Taoist manner. Perhaps the strict Confucian social ethic was made tolerable or balanced out only with the assistance of Taoist sarcasm, and life was made bearable only by the union of these two ways of thinking in every Chinese. If, however, human existence or human reason were unable any longer to show the way, then Buddhism was ultimately there to offer the spirit a refuge in the beyond, with all its advantages. It is said that formerly a person who wished to forge a career had to act as a Confucian, which is a view that yet prevails in the collective thought, although those concerned may no longer be conscious of it.

Religion in the strict sense was the popular religion, a mixture of the old folk religion with Buddhism, Taoism, and Confucianism, recruiting its divinities from the most diverse beliefs. Neither the popular priests nor the faithful could say—nor can they say even now-–to which religion or doctrine they adhered. This "religion," which can scarcely be defined, had its adherents among the common people, not the educated, who were instead devotees of philosophical Confucianism or Taoism.

As for other religions, there were reportedly three to four million Christians in China in 1949. Christianity had been spread by foreign churches, which exerted a critical influence on all church affairs. Islam, Lamaism, and both animist and animalistic beliefs were prevalent, primarily among the ethnic minorities. But a religion of redemption never developed in China itself. The absence of the idea of a single, almighty God—alien to the Chinese—is a fundamental difference from the Western notion of religion. (Although Buddhism, which came to China from India via Central Asia, was a religion of redemption, its main emphasis was on salvation rather than on giving meaning to life.) Life, the earth, nature, harmony, and human happiness, i.e., real, tangible things, were always at the center of Chinese thought—not an invisible God in heaven. This realism had its ideological foundation in Confucianism, which centered on man, not God. Man had equal status with heaven and earth and was not, as in Western Christian conceptions, dependent on God and his mercy. The Chinese philosopher Lin Yutang, born in America, captured this difference quite fittingly:

> Jesus was a romantic, Confucius a realist; Jesus was a mystic, Confucius a positivist. One can also say that Jesus was a humanitarian, a genius of human love, while Confucius was a humanistic genius . . . it is almost inconceivable to the Western mind that the relation between man and man could be fruitfully shaped without the idea of a supreme being, whereas it is just as astonishing to the Chinese why human beings should not be able to be decent to one another even without the thought of their direct relation through that third partner.[4]

For this reason, neither Confucius nor any of his disciples was exalted to the status of God. This also explains why China never produced a world religion: its own religious appurtenances consisted essentially of relics of the past in the form of what is known as "universism," with the worship of one's ancestors forming an integral part. Thus religion was neither necessary nor desirable for the Chinese, and that is one reason why Christianity never succeeded in recruiting a large following in China (remember that 4 million in 1949 constituted less than 1 percent of the population). Philosophical Confucianism gave the upper stratum of officials and literati a relatively closed body of thought that contained certain antireligious traits.

China was as areligious for the scholars of ancient China as it is for the educated in the China of today. This must be kept in mind when discussing today's religious policy. China's supreme power has always endeavored to keep religious activities under control so as not to jeopardize the unity and stability of the state, since religious sects and secret societies have been regularly at the head of peasant revolts. Religions were therefore approved and tolerated only as long as they supported the state and demonstrated themselves to be loyal. Religion was never regarded as a power above the state.

The "mission" of Christianity in China

Although the Christian mission in China was not a totally negative experience for China, Christianity has borne the brunt of antireligious incidents in China in this century, and for good reason. Displayed against the backdrop of the missions' positive contributions—to cultural exchange, education, the alleviation of poverty, and the growth of society—is the picture of foreigners who used missionary "incidents" as an excuse to implement their gunboat policy and to be contemptuous of Chinese customs and way of life. Even today, many Chinese associate the missionaries with China's national weakness in the nineteenth and first half of the twentieth centuries, and identify them with the exercise of foreign power in China.

With the Treaty of Tianjin (1858), the Christian missionaries obtained a privileged position. In all of their actions, the religionists were conscious of having the armed protection of Western powers behind them. Foreigners, who possessed the privileges of extraterritoriality, exacted harsh penalties from their opponents and demanded high compensation. Incidents arising from the Christians' ignorance of Chinese customs and the locals' intolerance of the religionists multiplied in the latter half of the nineteenth century, sometimes resulting in violent unrest. Where the missionaries experienced "difficulties," foreign gunboats often arrived to intimidate the local population or authorities, to demand reparations, or to win special privileges.

German missionaries alone were responsible for many ugly incidents: they labeled the graves and temples of ancestors "superstitious," and had them torn down in Shandong; they converted Buddhist temples into churches; and they used the murder of two German missionaries in Shandong as a pretext for occupying the city of Qingdao with German troops as a colonial "protectorate." The hate of foreigners finally exploded in the "Boxer Rebellion" in 1900. The atrocities of the "Christian" powers in this war, and later in World War I and the Treaty of Versailles,* only served to strengthen the "anti-Christian movement." This movement subsequently became an important part of the "Fourth of May movement" in 1919, out of which the Communist Party of China was born. The Communists still see themselves as part of the tradition of the Fourth of May movement, which was areligious and which sought an intellectual and cultural renewal for China.

The German sinologist Richard Wilhelm (1873–1930), who himself spent decades as a priest and missionary in China, describes the negative aspects of the Christian mission in China in his work *Die Seele Chinas* (The Soul of China): condemnation and discrediting of Chinese beliefs and religious practices (such as stigmatizing the ancestor cult as "idolatry"); development of the profitable "coolie trade" (a commerce in coolies for the battlefields of World War I); efforts to tie China to Western values and, thus, to the West through Christianity, etc.[5] Since this outlook inspired disgust in the population at large, those Chinese who associated themselves with the mission were for the most part outcasts of society, or persons who expected material rewards. The missions did indeed provide financial rewards, free board, and schooling, and behind the missions stood the Western powers, a quality equally as alluring to some.

---

*The Treaty awarded the German colony to the Japanese against the will of the Chinese.

Modern Chinese religious policy to 1979

After the founding of the People's Republic, the faithful who were ready to accept the new order and to help in reconstruction received an offer of collaboration. Freedom of religious belief (like the freedom to profess no religion) was set down formally in the constitution, but religious associations had to extricate themselves from foreign influence and were no longer permitted to receive outside aid. The lands and institutions of church organizations became state property. The influence and margin of freedom of religions were restricted by placing the education and social welfare sectors of the religions under the control of the state. Foreign missionaries were expelled.

In 1951, a Bureau for Religious Affairs, attached to the State Council, was established to serve as a link between the government and the organizations of Buddhists, Moslems, Taoists, and Christians that came to be formed in the fifties.[6]

The constitution of the first Chinese Soviet Republic (1931) guaranteed religious freedom for all workers and peasants, and at the same time gave the right to conduct antireligious propaganda.[7] Mao Zedong had argued quite early on that religion should not be forbidden, but only restricted, for:

> The figures of the gods are the work of the peasants themselves and when the time comes the peasants will cast them aside with their own hands; there is no need for other people who would do this prematurely in their place. (Report on a Study of the Peasant Movement in Hunan.)[8]

In 1957, Zhou Enlai, at that time prime minister, declared

> . . . that religious belief is a question of the faith of the people and is not a political question. Regardless of whether a person is atheist or believer, materialist or idealist, all can support more or less the socialist system. In our Communist Party there are many party members who are peasants. . . . Many of them are functionaries in the community administration. Politically and ideologically, they quite thoroughly meet the demands of the socialist economic system and yet many of them are afraid of ghosts at night. Do you think that

Communists are not afraid of ghosts? I doubt it. People have the most diverse thoughts. As long as a person does not harm political life and economic production, we should leave him in peace. Religion will continue to exist for some time yet. Its future development depends on future conditions. But as long as human beings continue to be faced with ideological problems which they cannot explain and cannot solve, religious belief will be inevitable. . . . Our friends from religious circles need not worry whether religion can exist or not. According to the materialist conception there will be religion as long as society has not developed far enough to have eliminated the conditions for the existence of religion.[9]

But the "friends from religious circles" soon had cause for concern. The political ideological campaigns that became a regular occurrence after 1957 were extended to include religions and religious believers. Mao's early position and Zhou Enlai's view never became a reality in China. Complaints of discrimination and persecution began to be heard in 1958. A major Moslem uprising in northwestern China in 1958 and the Tibetan uprising in 1959 were also related to the religious question. The authorities dealt severely with the rebels at that time.

After bitter clashes within the party leadership in the early sixties, the "class struggle" was declared the focal point of all work. At the same time, a debate on the relationship between religion and superstition began. Initially only the latter came under assault. The central party newspaper, *Renmin ribao* (People's Daily), stated in August 1963 that beliefs that relied on superstition were not to be classified as religion, but as a "deception of the people," and therefore could count on no protection under the guidelines for freedom of religious belief.[10] The popular religion, Shamanism—as well as magic, occultism, geomancy, exorcism, and divination—came under the heading "superstition," but the "high religions" of Buddhism, Christianity, and Islam did not.

The Cultural Revolution brought about open and direct suppression of religious belief. The Red Guards drew no distinction between religion and superstition. Any methodology that saw the highest form of faith to lie not in Mao Zedong's thought but in another being was condemned. All religious shrines were closed. Religious writings, statues, and art works were destroyed, and the faithful harassed. Religion was one of the "four old things" (*si jiu*)—an old way of thinking, old culture, old customs, and old morals—that had to be eradicated, root and branch. This applied to the Han Chinese and the ethnic minorities alike.

For the latter, religious oppression was directly related to national oppression. Moslems were forced to raise hogs, and for a Hui (Moslem) eating pork became a criterion for acceptance into the party, the Communist Youth League, the army, and for access to jobs and promotions.[11] In some Moslem regions this led to rebellion.[12] In Tibet, which was the hardest hit, the Red Guards laid waste to 2,690 of the original 2,700 convents. Tibetans were forced to take part in the desecration and destruction of their own shrines and temples.[13] In the province of Yunnan, a Christian clergyman of Miao nationality was sentenced to death for practicing his faith in 1973. When the sentence was read, representatives of the Miao were forced to renounce their faith. Ironically, constitutionally guaranteed freedom of religion was still formally in effect at that time. In the West, it was believed that religion had been dealt a death blow in China.

The political liberalization that set in after the fall of the "Gang of Four" (led by Mao's widow Jiang Qing) and the ensuing discussion of China's political and economic future brought about a turn in religious policy. From 1979 onward, religions were once again permitted to organize. Religious activity was permitted, and churches, mosques, and temples were restored by the state and returned to the faithful. Priests, lamas, and imams were permitted to return from their work in the fields and factories or from prison. The principles of religious freedom from the fifties were again affirmed. The 1982 constitution went so far as to broaden the rights of religious exercise. Article 36 of this constitution states:

> The citizens of the People's Republic enjoy religious freedom.
>
> No organ of the state, no social organization, and no individual may force citizens to adhere or not to adhere to a religion, nor may they place any citizen at a disadvantage who does or does not adhere to a religion.
>
> The state protects normal religious activities. No one may use a religion to carry out activities that disrupt the public order, harm the physical health of the citizens, or undermine the state's education system.

> Religious organizations and religious affairs may be controlled by no foreign force.[14]

The 1982 constitution established the most far-ranging rights since the founding of the People's Republic. The 1954 constitution had merely stated that "every citizen has the right to believe or not to believe";[15] in 1978 the passage ". . . and the freedom to propagate atheism" was added.[16] (The latter phrase was annulled in 1982 as covert discrimination, presumably alluding to the Vatican and its efforts to make contact with the Catholic Church of China.) The new penal law of 1979 provided for punishment of state officials who prevent citizens from the legitimate exercise of religion.[17]

Although all these points represent an expansion of the legal provisions for religious freedom, the imprecisions in their formulation permit arbitrary encroachments on religious freedom and allow for the possibility of restricting these rights. What, after all, does "normal religious activities" mean? Who "disrupts" the "public order" and when? Or who undermines the state's education system, and how and when? Elastic paragraphs such as these enable the bureaucracy to drastically restrict religious freedom in political ideological campaigns such as the campaign against "spiritual pollution" (1983) or against "bourgeois liberation" (1987).

Religious policy today

Initially, Chinese scholars endeavored to disentangle theoretically the terms religion and superstition. The latter was to remain forbidden. Thus a seminal article in *Renmin ribao* in 1979 stated:

> The reverence for supernatural secret powers can be called superstition. Religion is indeed superstition, but it would be wrong to say that all superstition is religion. The different types of feudal superstition, for example, are not religion.[18]

By the fourth century B.C. a difference in thinking had developed between the learned class and the common people, especially under the influence of Confucianism. The former, all educated Confucianists, rejected the belief in the supernatural and used Confucian humanism and philosophical aspects of Taoism and Buddhism to form their world view. In the common people, the religious and preternatural aspects of Confucianism, Taoism, and Buddhism found their expression in the "folk religion," which was despised by the upper classes, who regarded themselves as enlightened.[19]

This dualism is still evident in the religious policy of today. The folk religion and the early forms of religion (including those of the ethnic minorities) are rejected as "superstitious." The Communist Party today regards itself as the "enlightened" element, and sees its mission as raising up the common people. Hence, this function is completely within the Confucian tradition. In this regard, the German sinologist Wolfgang Bauer noted cogently that the "outside world" and "superstition," with their opposite poles of "China" and "enlightenment," form the basic coordinates governing the attitude of the Chinese government to religion, both today and in traditional China.[20]

Thus, the equating of religion with superstition has historical grounds. This equation led during the Cultural Revolution to the condemnation and prohibition of all forms of religious activity as superstition. In the same article, it was stated that nonreligions in this sense are all forms of "feudalistic superstition" such as the practices of witches, quacks, rainmakers, exorcists, geomancers, soothsayers, and magicians. The world religions of Buddhism, Christianity, Islam, and, in its more philosophical form, Taoism, were the only accepted religions. Earlier forms of religion such as Shamanism, animatism, and animism remained forbidden as "superstitions" like the earlier popular religion.

This position has become less rigid in recent years; the early forms of religion such as those mentioned have in fact been classified as religions by at least some scholars when they apply primarily to the national minorities who still practice them. But the popular religion—which comprises ecstatic and exorcistic practices, as well as divination, oracles, and geomancy—remains largely banished. This also has its tradition: the popular religion has always been despised by the learned and officials, and combated by the Confucians.

The religious policy of the Chinese Communists is based today on the following tenets:

1. Religion is a historical product that can only be abolished under certain socioeconomic and other conditions such as spreading scientif-

ic and cultural knowledge. Because religion has existed for a long time, the party must also pursue a long-term and continuous religious policy.

2. Religion has to do with the believer's attitude toward life and is hence an ideological problem. Ideological questions can only be resolved by democratic methods, education, and correct upbringing, not through force and violence or by administrative means. Experience shows that the influence of religion declines as material conditions become better, political participation increases, and the level of education rises.

3. Religion is not only a question of the "masses" and the nation, but is also a nationality problem. As many members of ethnic minorities are adherents of a religion, the religious question therefore is directly tied in with the nationality question. The correct treatment of the religious question is therefore of major importance for the unity of the country, the solidarity of peoples, and international relations.

4. The religious question is not an acute problem in China. The contradictions between believers and nonbelievers are not a key point of conflict. Both groups can work together on a friendly basis, be patriots, and support the party and socialism. Therefore in dealing with religious questions, the communality of political and economic interests among peoples must be stressed rather than differences in faith.[21]

So far that is the official perspective, marked by tolerant and harmonious cooperation. In actuality, there are a multitude of problems that, while posing no peril to state power, nonetheless do challenge it.

There are two important phenomena today that the state is battling in the religious question: first, the attempts of local officials to place themselves above the policy of religious freedom and to obstruct certain permitted religious activities; and second, the attempts of religious circles to expand their influence even *against* state interests.[22] These efforts include attempts (especially in Moslem and Buddhist regions) to coerce people who do not or no longer believe in religion to resume their faith; to spend public money for temple festivals or the construction of new temples; or to incite the faithful against the party, state, or state policies such as family planning or marriages of persons who do not or no longer belong to one's religious group.

Despite decades of propaganda against "superstition" and despite all attempts to eliminate it during the Cultural Revolution, superstition is returning today in all its forms. This ranges from traditional sacrifices to ancestors and burials through soothsaying and geomancy (divination that selects building sites or grave sites on the basis of the composition of the soil, the topography, etc.) to violent conflicts between sects and the "restoration of the earlier system of oppression and exploitation of temples and cloisters." In a number of places there already seem to be more temples than in the forties.[23]

The Chinese press often reports on the "terribly high number of superstitious activities" in the villages.[24] Cities are also affected: in spring 1987, the trade-union newspaper *Gongren ribao* reported on a factory in the city of Xuzhou where the management had hired several exorcists and magicians to put an end to "inexplicable incidents" in the enterprise by "driving out spirits and demons." Production had to be stopped for several days because of the "driving-out ceremony." The police later discovered that the "inexplicable incidents" were only a deliberate, planned act of revenge on the part of a young worker against the plant management.[25]

The dilemma becomes clear enough: on the one hand the attempt to at least partially restore religious freedoms (insofar as they support the state and are controllable); and on the other hand the effort to block missionary attempts, the propagation of religious beliefs, the restoration of the former privileges of religious circles, and the expansion of the influence of religion. Outlawing the popular religion causes it to flourish underground, which makes it very difficult for the state to control.

Interestingly, the influence of religion and superstition is rapidly growing among the actively engaged "individual entrepreneurs" (independent business people and tradesmen), possibly due to a low level of education. Since the independents could not explain to themselves the genesis of profits and losses, they sacrificed to the "God of Wealth" and other gods, and prayed for good business.[26] In fact, I believe the probable cause is that the individual entrepreneurs belong to no state or collective unit (*danwei*) and are able to evade the network of state controls.

Recent discussions on the essence of religion

Chinese scholars are today endeavoring to come up with a more differentiated picture of religion after many years of its being referred to as simply the "oppressive instrument of the exploiting classes" and the "opium of the people." There is quite a broad variety of views, but three principal ones may be distinguished:

1. Although the doctrines and the rites of religions present the objective world in distorted form and are contrary to Marxism, and although religion has a narcotic effect, the practice of religion must be permitted in socialist society. Atheistic education must, of course, be reinforced to eliminate the influence of religion as rapidly as possible.

2. Under a socialist society, religions have another character that allows them to enter into an alliance with socialism. Religion *not only* functions as the opium for the people but also shows the suffering of mankind and man's struggle against that suffering. In China, religion has never been a political power that exercised control of the state; rather it has been practiced by believers in free self-determination. Nor has it ever become an instrument of the ruling classes and used for domination over the people. Since religions have existed in China for quite a long time, the state must guide the faithful and work against the negative influences of religion.

3. In the early phases of the great religions (Christianity, Judaism, Buddhism, and Islam), the positive elements far outweighed the negative factors. It was not until later that religion came to be misused by the ruling classes to oppress the people. Religions have enriched history, culture, art, architecture, and medicine. A reevaluation of religion must therefore be undertaken.[27]

An open debate and a more differentiated approach are to be welcomed, since together they constitute an important precondition for a greater measure of religious freedom. Earlier, it was only the negative character of religion that was stressed, but today some scholars interested in the topic see positive aspects. The first and second of the above three positions are thoroughly traditional: a position of tolerance and a position of guidance and control. The third position leaves the manner of approach open but cautiously calls for a reevaluation.

There have already been far-ranging attempts in this respect. For example, Zhao Fusan, the vice president of Chinese Academy of Social Sciences (*Zhongguo shehui kexue yuan*), has even rejected the Marxist theory of religion as the "opium of the people" as being too narrow. Its characterization as opium and as a tool of the ruling classes does not respect history, culture, and peoples' power to believe. Religion, he says, is an important component of the cultural history of peoples.[28] A positive assessment such as this, if it were to prevail, could lead to a more relaxed religious policy and eliminate the fear harbored by the faithful of belonging to a superstitious or reactionary faith; their loyalty to the state would therefore grow. On the other hand, this approach would make possible a freer development of religions. Less restriction of the exercise of religion would make more people believers. The Communist Party would then see this as a weakening of its own position.

Thus, the second position of those outlined above is the most likely one to determine the future of religions in China.

Religious policy and the question of national minorities

A large proportion of the roughly 70 million members of ethnic minorities belong to some religion, mainly Islam and Buddhism; Christianity also has influence among some minorities. The religious question is intimately linked to the nationality question—how closely was demonstrated by the uprisings of Uygur Moslems in the city of Kashgar in 1981[29] and of the Tibetan lamas in recent years.

A revival of religion is evident in minority regions, more conspicuously in the countryside than in the cities. A vigorous, lively religious activity is discernible everywhere, but especially in Islamic and Buddhist regions. Sacred writings (the Koran, the Bible, the Daodejing, etc.) have been officially published.[30] Mosques and temples have been restored mainly on the initiative and with the resources of the faithful. In the Hui (the largest Moslem minority) regions in northwest China, whole city districts have built their own mosques. The names of all donors were listed on large wall posters. Hui respondents declared almost without exception to the author that their greatest desire was to make a pilgrimage to Mecca; many took leisure-time jobs to save money for this trip. The desire for an Islamic upbringing for their children and for their receiving instruction in the rules of the Koran is considerable. In Tibet as well, religion has enjoyed a revival among the youth.

None of this is surprising; religion cannot be simply suppressed, and experiences in China have confirmed this. Religion is a part of a national culture and national identity for many ethnic minorities. Professing one's religion means profession of one's own nationality, and demonstrates a heightened awareness of nationality.

The official policy is that the authorities are not to interfere in the religious affairs of minorities as long as state affairs and the education system are not affected. But the line is difficult to draw. Among the Islamic Hui, the mullahs are more frequently listened to than the party secretaries. And party membership and religious membership are still considered incompatible. The fact that the party warns against participation of party cadres in religious or "superstitious" activities (which is evidently increasing in minority regions)[31] shows that religion still holds some power of attraction, even for officials.

But a distinction must be drawn between party members of Han nationality and those of national minorities. The latter must "not be rejected" if they have not yet completely severed their ties with their religious beliefs; rather, they "must be helped" (through "ideological education") to "raise their political consciousness." Only those who incite religious fanaticism and work against the principles of the party in the name of religion should be removed from the party.[32]

Functionaries from minority regions are faced with a dilemma: they are expected to sever themselves from the religion of their nationality. But if they no longer believe in the religious doctrines and rites but reject them, and refuse to participate in the ceremonies held by members of their nationality (weddings, funerals, and other solemnities), they soon find themselves rejected by the members of their ethnic group. The minority cadres, who are always potentially pursuing the wrong course, certainly will find it difficult to decide how they should behave and what attitude the party actually desires of them. They thus run the risk (as in Moslem regions) of isolating themselves from the majority of the believers. This puts them in a permanent conflict of conscience between allegiance to the party and to the religious population. The Chinese press frequently refers to the growing trend of punishing those who no longer believe in religion by "expelling them from their membership in a nationality," indicating that for many minorities, nationality questions and the religion question are identical.[33]

Prospects

Religion in China is seen as something alien, as something that has come from outside and that is sometimes a threat to the state; as something that gains influence especially in times of internal weakness; as a counterpoint to higher Confucian morality—these traditional basic structures are still to a certain extent operative today in the official attitude toward religions. Even though state intervention in religious matters would be hardly conceivable in the West, from the historical perspective of China it seems almost logical, since religious groups have often been the center of incursions into state power. The experience with Christianity in the nineteenth and twentieth centuries showed the Chinese how religion can be used by foreign powers to weaken China. Accordingly, the overtures of foreign churches are still today regarded with suspicion.

Yet deference to foreign nations in the interest of the political and economic open-door policy of China is probably a decisive factor in allowing expanded religious activity. The Chinese leadership is trying to focus the faithful of all religions on the objective of developing China, urging believers and nonbelievers alike to work together to the good of the country.

But what if the party begins to lose the "ideological struggle"? This could very well lead to continual friction and oppositions between the party and the faithful.

Theoretically, cooperation between religious circles and Communists is not ruled out despite the antagonism between the two as long as the latter respect and protect the freedom of religious belief and the former do not work against the interests of the party. But since these interests can be interpreted in different ways, relations between the faithful and the Communists can hardly remain free of conflict. Religious leaders such as the Dalai Lama therefore are seeking new interpretations to allow for mutual cooperation. The Dalai Lama sees, for example, strong similarities between the goals of the Marxists and of the Buddhists, and therefore the possibility for "peaceful coexistence" and cooperation, and even mutual enrichment.[34]

By definition, religion must endeavor to spread the faith. Religious freedom in the Western sense is conducive to the spread of religion. But if religion must subordinate itself to the interest of the state power, and this interest is directed against spread of religion, then there is no religious freedom *in this sense*.

8

The Tibet Question

The unrest in Tibet in the autumn of 1987 and the springs of 1988 and 1989 once again focused world attention on the Tibet question, which is without a doubt a key issue in the nationality policy of the People's Republic of China. The following does not pretend to provide an exhaustive analysis of this problem, something that has already been adequately done by others.[1] The Chinese arguments and methods in Tibet need be neither justified nor excused, but China should also not be overhastily condemned. This discussion shall attempt instead to illuminate a few aspects of the problem to help explain Chinese conduct, something that is important to understanding the Tibet question.

A brief history of Tibet

Circa sixth century A.D., the Tibetans began major military incursions into China, India, and Burma. In the ninth century, the Tibetan kingdom collapsed due to internal struggles, and the Chinese Tang (618–907) dynasty regained the regions that had been lost to the Tibetans. It was the Mongols who first brought about a closer relationship between Tibet and China, when they conquered both China and Tibet in the thirteenth century and founded the Yuan dynasty (1279–1368). The Yuan emperors were recognized by both parties as the overlords of Tibet, but the Lamas governed Tibet's internal affairs. The relationship between Tibet and China continued essentially unchanged during the Ming dynasty (1368–1644), which ended Mongol rule, and the Qing dynasty (1644–1911).

There were some incidents that helped to strengthen the Chinese position during this period: following the disturbances after the death of the fifth Dalai Lama in 1682, the Manchu emperors sent a military expedition to Tibet to restore order. In 1720 the Tibetans appealed to the Chinese army for help against the invading Dzungars. After a successful campaign, the Chinese emperor concluded a treaty with the Dalai Lama, in which Tibet came under Chinese hegemony.

As a result of internal unrest in the eighteenth century, a Chinese garrison was sent to Tibet and two civilian officials (*ambans*) were installed as permanent agents and inspectors of the emperor's court. In the late eighteenth century, the Nepalese Gurkhas twice attacked Tibet. The local government asked for assistance from Chinese troops, who drove out the invaders. As a result, all external contacts of Tibet were placed under Chinese control and foreigners were refused entry, under the pretext that the British had supported the Gurkhas.

Up to 1912, then, Tibet remained a protectorate which—as was traditional in the Chinese policy toward the non-Han nations—continued to be governed by Tibetans. This traditional policy provided that the ruler of a nation or a region would officially place himself under the Chinese emperor, who would then officially bestow an office on the ruler and (as in the case of Tibet) furnish a Chinese official at his side. This was initially a military, and later a civil, governor.

In the beginning of this century, both England and Russia strove for greater influence in Tibet as part of their rivalry in Central Asia. In 1903–1904, Great Britain tried to reach an agreement with Tibet by direct intervention. After battles in which the Tibetans suffered heavy losses, an accession was wrested from the Tibetan government, which fixed the boundary between Sikkim and Tibet and conceded certain trading rights to Great Britain. Since the British had not included the Chinese in this agreement, the latter insisted on recognition of Chinese sovereignty over Tibet during the negotiations for a British-Chinese treaty wherein the British formally recognized China's hegemony over Tibet. In the Russian-British Accord of 1907, the Russians pledged to deal with Tibet only through the Chinese government. The Chinese endeavored to strengthen their claim to sovereignty by heavier military control over Tibet, and in 1910 they even marched into Lhasa and proscribed all contact between Tibetans and British.

During the course of the Chinese Revolution of 1911, there were armed conflicts between Tibetans and Chinese, who were driven out of Tibet with the help of Nepal in 1912. The thirteenth Dalai Lama declared Tibet independent of the Chinese government. Although the Chinese government continued to assert its sovereignty over Tibet, the British would acknowledge only a "suzerainty."

Internal turmoil in China, and then the Japanese invasion, prevented further political and military ties between Tibet and China. Tibet's attempt to take advantage of the Chinese situation by seeking international recognition during the 1940s foundered, and not a single nation would acknowledge Tibet as an independent state. In 1950, the Chinese People's Liberation Army marched into Tibet, and in 1951 an agreement was signed guaranteeing autonomy to the Tibetans, as well as the continued existence of their institutions and the rights of the Dalai Lama. At the same time, it was declared that Tibet was—and is—a part of China.

In the mid-1950s the Chinese sought to enforce their domain in Tibet, sometimes with violence; there was increasing unrest and resistance among the Tibetans, and in 1959, open revolts broke out. The Dalai Lama led a large number of Tibetans into exile in India. In the succeeding years, especially during the Cultural Revolution, all forms of Tibetan independence and political structures were shattered, and the monasteries were closed and destroyed. The plan was to pacify Tibet by abolishing its culture and persecuting dissidents.

Not until the early 1980s, when the Chinese state (hitherto having little or no information as to the actual affairs in Tibet) delved into the Tibet situation, were the Tibetans promised more independence in political, economic, and cultural respects. The success of this has been limited, however, since local officials are reluctant to institute reforms; thus Tibet lags behind other regions. Wu Jinghua (until 1988 the Party secretary of Tibet, and a member of the Yi nationality) was even called openly the "Lama-secretary" by the other local officials, because he attended major religious ceremonies to demonstrate his support for religious policy in Tibet.[2]

The concept of "state" in China

In 1911 and 1949 Tibet attempted to make itself independent from China. The status of Tibet within the community of nations was therefore a controversial question for a time in international law, even though not one country ever recognized Tibet as an independent state, and today Tibet is regarded in international law as a part of the People's Republic of China.

This is not sufficient, however, to explain the intervention of Chinese troops in 1950. There are two factors that have not yet been taken into account in Western discussions of the Tibet question. China clearly proceeds from a different conception of nation and state when fixing its borders than do the modern Western nation-states. Unlike in Europe, where today's nation-states were formed only in the last two centuries, the Chinese empire has existed for over 2,000 years. The territory of today's China has been Chinese territory for many centuries. The historical inclusion of an area as a part of China was and is considered by the Chinese to be as strong a criterion as was the drawing of the borders of the young European national states.

Western principles of international law derive from the European legal philosophy as it developed in the nineteenth century, a period in which all the major states of Europe exercised a colonial rule over many peoples. European legal principles therefore cannot be translated directly and straightforwardly to Chinese circumstances. To the Chinese, all peoples who live in the territory of today's China are considered part of the Chinese people. Thus, in the official view, Tibetans also have belonged to China for quite some time. It was the weakness of the Qing dynasty and pressure and influence from foreign powers that were responsible for the severance of large areas from China in the nineteenth and early twentieth centuries.

A similar situation exists with the Mongolian People's Republic. Sun Yat-sen, the founder of the Chinese republic in 1911, called for a new national identity and a "new nationalism" of all the peoples of China to strengthen the country and to bring about a national renaissance. He continued to regard what is today the Mongolian People's Republic as a part of the Chinese nation even after it was separated from the Chinese empire, although the Mongols had other ideas. Even today, the Mongolian People's Republic is not recognized by Taiwan as an independent state, but is considered part of China.

Thus the ideological basis for the reincorporation of Tibet in 1950 was based on both the view that all the peoples and ethnic groups who had lived on Chinese territory up to 1911 were part of the Chinese nation, and on the fact that China's weakness at the time was unable to prevent the "defection" of some territories. The Chinese concept of law therefore equates the territorial principle with the national principle, a point on which the Guomindang in Taiwan and the Communist Party of the People's Republic of China are, as of now, largely in agreement.

In 1950 the Communists attempted to revalidate this principle of law with the reincorporation of Tibet. At the same time they wanted to demonstrate that the era of the "ailing man in the East," as China had long been called, was past. China, which has claimed sovereignty over Tibet since 1911, felt justified in reincorporating a territory that had almost been lost on account of "imperialist influences."

It is vital to remember that several foreign powers in this century (especially England and Russia) made repeated attempts to tear strategically important territories such as Tibet or Xinjiang away from China. These regions were attractive not only because they possess invaluable deposits of raw materials, but also because their severance would have made the invasion, possible dismemberment, and colonial control of China much easier.

Tibet in modern history

The Chinese had effectively lost their grip in Tibet by the end of the Qing dynasty in 1911, owing to both internal and external weaknesses. The struggle between Great Britain and Russia for hegemony in Central Asia already had made Tibet a bone of contention between these two powers in the nineteenth century.[3] This notwithstanding, Tibet has been mentioned in China's constitutions since 1912 as a "neighboring territory outside the provincial organization" of the rest of China and placed under the "Mongolian and Tibetan Affairs Bureau" (from 1914 on, Ministry, and from 1927 on, Commission for Mongolia and Tibet).[4] But as for the Western colonial powers, Tibet was considered part of the "British sphere of interest." Since 1904, it had been in fact a representative of Great Britain who decided who could enter Tibet. A British journalist wrote in the 1940s:

> As was the case with many other places in the world, Britain did not think first and foremost of tapping the wealth and the potential of the

country in which it had ensured its paramount influence. It was sufficient for Britain that no other country could do this. This attitude was in consonance with the wishes of the ruling priest caste in Tibet who endeavored to keep at bay all Western influence so as not to jeopardize their rule. Thus Tibet has to this very day remained a vast area of totally untouched riches which could be transformed into a Garden of Eden with the means of modern technology. It has remained an empty desert because this suited the objectives of British policy.[5]

The German secret diplomatic agent Filchner made the following report on his Tibet research:

Tibet played a quite unique role in the past in the struggles of interest between England and Russia and is still playing that role today. . . . The gaze of the whole world is therefore rightly and expectantly turned toward the Tibetan highlands, this witch's cauldron of Asia. For the Anglo-Indian government it is of crucial importance to create a well fortified stronghold in Tibet on India's northern front in its conflict with Russia. England has oriented its policy in Lhasa wholly with this in mind.[6]

It was primarily the violation of the interests of this great colonial power that shook the Western powers in 1950, since with Tibet incorporated into the Chinese state polity it was abruptly lost to Western interests. China was also quite conscious of the deleterious effects of Western influence in an independent Tibet, from whence China (deprived of a natural border in the southwest) could be easily harassed.[7] This vulnerability helps to explain why China has doggedly defended its claim to the possession of Tibet since the Qing dynasty.

Of course, this is not to say that the Tibetans do not have the right to independence. The Chinese government imposed its presumptive right by force in 1950 and subordinated Tibetan aspirations to independence to China's own legal claim. The controversy over whether China was justified in doing so cannot be decided here. It is more important to endeavor to explain the Chinese position from another perspective, since from a Western standpoint it is a genuine conundrum. In Western legal terms it was an outright occupation, in Chinese terms the "restoration of a historically unambiguous right'' which, due to external circumstances China had not been able to exercise for some time.

From the standpoint of international law, the principle of self-determination is a key factor to both the nationality problem in general and the Tibet case in particular. The actual purport of this principle continues to be a matter of international contention. For a long time the view prevailed that the principle of self-determination of peoples was more a moral or a political postulate than a principle of law. It was later declared a fundamental human right consequent to the liberation of the colonial peoples. But difficulties quickly arose when attempts were made to apply the principle of self-determination in practice. The people, it was said, must decide. But who are the people? And which people have the right to self-determination? If the dangerous dismemberment of states is to be avoided while this principle is being translated into practice, then an institution that decides such questions is needed. A UN declaration from 1970 states:

> On the basis of the principle of equality and self-determination of peoples in the charter of the United Nations, all peoples have the right to freely determine, without outside interference, their political status and to pursue their own path of economic social and cultural development, and every state is bound to respect this right in accordance with the provisions of the Charter.[8]

However, UN resolution 1514 (XV) contains a protective clause for existing states, stating that "any attempt aimed at partial or total disruption of the national unity and territorial integrity of a country is incompatible with the aims and principles of the charter."[9] It was feared that an unrestricted recognition of the principle of self-determination would encourage secessionist movements and could result in the disintegration of existing states. The UN therefore neither advocates nor supports any action aimed at the division or destruction of the territorial integrity or the political unity of sovereign and independent states that "are guided by the principle of equality and self-determination."[10]

The UN introduced the criterion of "legitimacy" to define whether a country is guided by this principle. Accordingly, a state with a government that represents all the people of a specific territory, regardless of race, color or creed, is legitimate. Separatist movements in states that conform to this principle of legitimacy are neither supported nor approved by the UN. On the other hand, a state that does not meet this criterion can count on no protection from the UN against such movements. A state's refusal to permit an equitable say in the exercise of its sovereign authority (but not simply the denial of national and cultural autonomy) can be considered justification for a people's demand for self-determination. This view is also shared by the Chinese government,[11] and indeed the international community has so far accepted that China had this "legitimacy" and that Tibet is therefore a part of China.

Tibet's prospects

Tibet has been a victim of the crossfires and waves in recent Chinese history. Indeed, the oft-cited "Tibetan hate of the Chinese" stems largely from the Cultural Revolution, in which the Tibetan culture was ravaged and partially destroyed.[12] (These excesses affected not only the Tibetans but also all of China's nationalities, although they were especially stormy in Tibet.)

In spite of recent liberalization, petty and bureaucratic behavior today is still widespread among many officials—especially those of minority origin—in minority regions. Minority officials who defended the interests of their nationality found themselves in the crossfire of criticism in the political campaigns in the fifties, sixties, and seventies. This made them very cautious and especially bureaucratic. Many centrally conceded freedoms therefore made only slow and limited headway in Tibet. Waves of criticism in Beijing soon assumed the dimensions of persecutions in Tibet, leading to extreme discontent with the local bureaucracies.

The unrest of 1987, 1988, and 1989 has at least resulted in the Chinese state being more open to issues of self-government for Tibet and to negotiations with the Dalai Lama. In March 1988, for example, it was resolved to make Tibetan the primary language of public affairs in Tibet. Thus, Han cadres working in Tibet must know or learn the Tibetan language. In September, the late Panchen Lama (the second highest religious ruler of the Tibetans and vice chairman of the Standing Committee of the National People's Congress) announced that a committee was being formed under his leadership, with the professed goal of assuring ''self-government of religion'' in Tibet and precluding administrative interference in the religious affairs of all Tibetans in China.[13] But the difficulty of implementing such a decision is shown by the fact that in March 1989, one year after the first decision to make Tibetan the primary language of public affairs in Tibet, the party committee of Tibet decided this again. Evidently nothing was done in this year to realize this decision.

In the meantime, the Chinese state has also retreated from its demand that the Dalai Lama, should he return to China, must reside in Beijing, instead leaving it to his discretion as to where he will live.

There are few who would be surprised that many Tibetans feel that the only way that their culture will be able to develop freely is for them to have their own state. Protests and demands for independence are able to draw the attention of the world and of Beijing to the problem of Tibet, and may even bring about improvements over the long term. But in real terms, China cannot and will not ever give Tibet its independence. Not only would that jeopardize China's national security policy, it also would mean a loss of face for China, something that no leadership could afford without serious consequences.

Following the Tibetan protests in 1989, Deng Xiaoping declared that China was ready to negotiate anytime and anywhere, and that *all points* would be negotiated—apart from the question of the independence of Tibet from China. The Dalai Lama, too, does not require independence, but realistically has proposed that Tibet should get the status of an autonomous region associated with China that democratically administers its own affairs. Beijing's only role would be to represent Tibet in foreign affairs. A limited number of Chinese soldiers could be stationed in Tibet until it became a neutral zone. In other words, the Dalai Lama wants to revert to a state that Tibet, in its history with China, has held for a long time.

Although this position has not yet prevailed, it does make concessions to the Chinese government. So far it is a good starting point for negotiations for both sides, although it is a claim that is unlikely to be accepted in its totality by the Chinese leadership. But it should not be forgotten that a democratic solution to the Tibet question will not be possible until the political conditions in China themselves undergo massive changes.

9

Prospects

How to sum up the nationality policy of the People's Republic of China?

The first and most important factor in the policy was the recognition—for the first time in Chinese history—of the various ethnic groups as independent nationalities. Both the early fifties and the late eighties have seen some basic steps taken to give equal legal status and rights to all nationalities. New written languages have been created for a number of minorities who had none previously. In many regions, an industrial base may have been created and educational and health care institutions established.

But since the end of the fifties, progress has stagnated in most regions—both minority and Han—because of misguided political economic policies, for which the Communist Party must bear the responsibility. In periods of political campaigns, particularly the Great Leap Forward and the Cultural Revolution, there was massive suppression of nationalities and even attempts to assimilate them forcibly.

All regions and nationalities had to bear the brunt of the political campaigns, the mistakes in economic and social policy, and their consequences. But there was one crucial difference in the effects on the Han and the minorities. The ethnic minorities considered the policies of the Communist Party, which had resulted in oppression, discrimination, and coercive action, to be national oppression by the Han and "their party." The Han Chinese, on the other hand, placed the blame on the Communist Party or a faction of the party leadership. Hence the political mistakes of the Communist Party of China in national minority regions were doubly grave because they led to, or reinforced, national contradictions and conflicts. All the old resentments against the Han were revived and national resistance intensified. For a long time, an objective policy of national oppression was pursued, although subjectively this may not have been the intention.

Rooting out minority mistrust of the Han will be a long and difficult process. It has evolved over the course of history, and received new sustenance from the political movements of the last few decades. But the time of seemingly patient reception of all that is mandated by Beijing has passed. The Communist Party tried to reestablish a basis of trust by designing economic policies and by granting broader autonomy in some spheres. The economic policy implemented in the early eighties, and accompanying improvements in material living conditions throughout the country, did restore some of the party's prestige.

Clear demands for independence from China existed first only in Tibet, if for no other reason than that the nationalities were so dispersed in other regions that they did not have the means to unite for secession. But now also Xinjiang and Inner Mongolia are seeing such tendencies. An official report lists seven known separatist organizations of different nationalities in Xinjiang. They all call themselves "Turkic" movements and have connections to pan-Turkic organizations in the Soviet Union and Turkey. Wang Enmao, the former party secretary of Xinjiang, called those separatist tendencies the "greatest danger for Xinjiang."[1]

Secessionist demands pose no serious threat to the state, but they could multiply over the long term if minority demands for economic and cultural development and for more autonomy are not met. Although the Chinese leadership is attempting to find the right formula, in recent years there have been signs of stagnation and hardening in policies on minorities. Economic liberalization has led to the desire of various nationalities for a more independent development. The party leadership sees this as a growing threat to its power, and to the unity of the nation.

There are today essentially three factors that undermine the national and cultural identity of minorities. First, lower-level officials often obstruct even the implementation of centrally determined policies. These are not only Han but also minority officials who, on the basis of their experience over the past decade, have become especially apprehensive, bureaucratic, and conservative. They are continually interfering in trivial ways in the lives of the minorities and creating tensions. Since they do not defend the interests of their nationalities they are seen as representatives of the Han and not of their own ethnic group.

A second factor is "Han chauvinism" (*hanzuzhuyi*), which finds expression in contempt for and discrimination against the habits, customs, and culture of the minorities. But the gravest undermining factor is the deficient sensitivity that permeates the bureaucracy all the way from the central authorities down to the local level in searching for a way to integrate modernization and development on the one hand, and in deference to the customs and cultural identity of the ethnic groups on the other. The opening up of minority regions and their settlement by Han Chinese in disregard of ethnic cultural ways has caused a kind of cultural shock among the smaller groups, and among the major groups, resistance and rebellion. An unintended byproduct of this trait is the further assimilation of the minorities.

The 1982 constitution and the law of autonomy of 1984 are a long way from meeting the demands of many minorities for greater autonomy, despite the verbal concession of wide-ranging rights. Local minorities still have practically no influence on Han migration into their areas, on their own self-administration in the true sense of the word, and on self-determination of economic and cultural development (even wholly within the constitution), although these laws formally establish the widest-ranging set of rights since the founding of the People's Republic. The future attitude of minorities will ultimately depend on how China will develop politically. Liberalization of economic policies must lead to political reform that allows minorities the possibility of more independent development, improvement in their living conditions, and conservation of their cultural identity.

The social mobilization that goes hand in hand with development will doubtless make for potential politicization along ethnic cultural lines, i.e., a nationalism driven by rising expectations and frustrations. Social discontent, even to the point of separatist tendencies among the major groups, will grow if promises of development are not met or if there is no steady and fundamental improvement in living standards, and if there are attempts to oppress and to curtail cultural identity (e.g., through the increased immigration of Han Chinese into minority regions).

The number of nationalities could be diminished over the long term by deliberate linguistic and cultural assimilation, which would result in increased uniformity among the population and in minorities renouncing their own and assuming Han culture and language instead. The minor nationalities especially, as well as those groups that are either dispersed through the regions or living as enclaves in Han regions, are unable to offer resistance to such a policy of assimilation as has been practiced more or less openly since the late fifties. All party assurances to the contrary, the current "soft" policy of national integration seems to be traveling the path of assimilation among the smaller ethnic groups. It is certainly contestable whether this is a necessary process within the broader evolution of society as a whole, or whether it ought in general terms to be avoided. Majorities usually do not seriously consider the latter possibility, especially in the case of smaller groups, and those affected are usually not even asked if the policy meets with their desires. The apparent "backwardness" of the smaller minorities must, so goes the argument, be abolished by "development" in what is purported to be their own interests to bring them up to the standards of the majority. Generally, small ethnic groups are broken up by this "civilizing" process, as experience worldwide testifies.

Economic reforms alone will not produce fundamental changes in nationality policy and in relations among the national minorities. The development of economic liberties and an "open door" policy demonstrated clearly that the political system in China is lumbering and antiquated. Economic conditions affect political ones, and a centralized, monopolized political system cannot coexist with a decentralized economic system. Instead, decentralization of the economic system leads to decentralization of the political one—i.e., a challenge to the power monopoly of the party. In the case of national minorities, the party leadership fears that such a challenge will endanger the nation as a whole.

The brutal reaction of the party leadership to the demonstrations and protests in Chinese cities in the spring of 1989 shows just how unwilling the Old Guard is to make any concessions. It can only be hoped that in times to come liberal forces dedicated to carrying out political reforms will rise to power in the party.

Only extensive liberalization, linked to democratization, may encourage a rethinking of the minority policy. Perhaps then the reformers will realize that the standards of the Han cannot be applied to national minorities. But without true liberalization, the party leadership will continue to react with pressure and force to every attempt by minorities to gain more independence. In the long run such a hard line and its effects may be the ultimate block to the unity of the country.

Notes

Chapter 1

1. On this question see *Gesellschaft für Bedrohte Völker* (1982).
2. See *Newsweek Magazine*, September 21, 1981: 16ff.
3. *Gesellschaft für Bedrohte Völker* (1982), 224.
4. On this point see Biegert (1981); Münzel (1981).
5. *Die Welt* (November 15, 1980); on this point see also Roberts (1979).
6. Chaliand (1980).
7. *West-Papua* (1983).
8. Schild (1981), pp. 31ff.
9. *Asiaweek*, January 25, 1980.
10. On this point see Azrael (1958); Allworth (1971); "Nationalitätenfragen" (1971); d'Encausse (1979); Revesz (1979); Brunner and Meissner (1982); Krag (1983).
11. Brunner and Meissner (1982), p. 152.
12. Ibid., p. 171.
13. Theodorson (1964), pp. 1ff.; Fleischmann (1976); Heidhues (1983), pp. 145ff.
14. On this point see *Frankfurter Allgemeine*, December 12, 1978.
15. On this point see *Kunstadter* 2 (1976): 369ff.
16. Hero (1977), pp. 1ff.
17. See for example *Die Welt*, June 6, 1979.
18. Razon and Hensman (1976).
19. Fremery 7 (1983): 311.
20. See *Far Eastern Economic Review*, June 30, 1978.
21. *Beijing Review* 18 (1972): 8.
22. *Beijing Review* 10 (1972): 13.
23. See for example Morrock (1972); Chen (1977); Han (1978).
24. For more on this problem, see Pimenoff (1973), pp. 23ff.
25. Francis (1965), p. 124.
26. Ibid., p. 206.
27. Thus: Wirth (1945), p. 347; Kurzrock (1974), p. 74f.; Nairn et al. (1977); Wentzel (1985).

28. *Zhongguo 1982 nian renkou pucha ziliao* (1985), pp. 218ff.

29. *Renmin ribao*, November 12, 1987.

30. Thus, in the seventies the prominent Soviet journalist Victor Louis predicted the collapse of China as a consequence of internal conflicts between the nationalities. Though Louis' arguments were untenable, they concealed a Soviet desire for a weakening of China through its ethnic minorities. Cf. Louis (1977).

31. *Minzu yuwen lunji* (1981); *Minzu yuwen yanjiu wenji* (1982); *Minzu yuwen yanjiu* (1983); *Zhongguo minzu yuwen lunwenji* (1986); *Zhongguo shaoshu minzu yuyan* (1987).

32. Eberhard found that 800 tribes and ethnic groups are listed under separate names in Chinese historical sources (Eberhard 1942, p. 411). On the general problem see also Lattimore (1962); Dreyer (1976), pp. 7ff.; Bauer (1980).

33. Li Gi (1981), p. 102.

34. Sun Yat-sen (1927), p. 24. On this point see also Hsü (1933), p. 168; Sun Yat-sen (1953), 180; Liu Qinbin (1981); *Minzu yanjiu* 6 (1981): p. 12ff.

35. Quoted in *China Handbook* (1949), p. 74.

36. Chiang Kai-shek and May Ling (1945), pp. 84, 94; Chiang Kai-shek (1947), pp. 39ff.

37. For a discussion of this point see also *Lishi yanjiu* 5 (1980); *Beijing shifan daxue xuebao* 6 (1981): 1; *Guangming ribao*, (May 25, 1981); *Minzu yanjiu* 5 (1981): 76ff; *Xinjiang shehui kexue* 1 (1981): 42ff; *Zhongyang minzu xueyuan xuebao* 2 (1981); *Zhongguo minzu guanxi shi lunwenji* (1982); *Zhongguo minzu guanxi shi lunwen xuanji* (1983); Weng Dujian (1984).

38. See also *Zhongguo jindaishi ziliao xuanbian*, vol. 1 (1977); *Taiping tianguo geming shiji* (1978); *Xinan minzu xueyuan xuebao* 2 (1981): 24ff.

39. *Guizhou minzu yanjiu* (1981), 32ff; *Minzu tuanjie* (1981): 5ff; *Yunnan xinhai geming ziliao* (1981).

40. *Zhongguo jindaishi gao* (1978); *Xinjiang jianshi* (1980). For more details see Willoughby (1920), pp. 257ff.; Sao (1965). On Tibet see Filchner (1942); Burman (1979), pp. 10ff.; *Xizang yanjiu* 3 (1982). On Southwest China see Hosie (1972).

41. See *Minzu yanjiu* 2 (1958): 13.

42. For more detail see Franke (1967), p. 445ff.; Wang Shuwu (1981), p. 87ff.

43. *Sixiang zhanxian* 3 (1980): 21.

44. *Zhongnan minzu xueyuan xuebao* (1981): 23ff.; on this point see also Bai Shouyi (1981).

45. See Zhou Liangxiao (1981), pp. 97ff. There are basically three views on this point today: a) The principal trend of friendship and cooperation; b) the principal trend of belligerent conflicts; c) the principle trend of common development of China. See also on this point Bai Shouyi (1981); *Renmin ribao*, December 29, 1981; *Zhongyang minzu xueyuan xuebao* 2 (1981): 9ff., 16ff.; *Zhongyang minzu xueyuan xuebao* 4 (1981): 42.

46. *Zhongyang minzu xueyuan xuebao* 1 (1982): 33ff.

47. *Zhongyang minzu xueyuan xuebao* 3 (1982): 21.

48. On this discussion see also *Xinjiang shehui kexue* (1981): 42ff.; *Zhongguo Shi yanjiu Dongtai* 10 (1981): 1ff.; *Zhongguo shehui kexue* 5 (1982): 143ff.

Chapter 2

1. Also see, e.g., McMillen (1979, pp. 181ff.); Dreyer (1976, pp. 205ff.);

Burman (1979, pp. 141ff.); Dreyer (1968); Hyer and Heaton (1968); *China News Analysis* 721 (1968).

2. On this point see: *Renmin ribao*, August 9, 1966; in German: *Beschluss des ZK der KPCh über die Grosse Proletarische Kulturrevolution* (1966); other documents in Schickel (1969); Ding Wang (1967); *Wichtige Dokumente der Grossen Proletarischen Kulturrevolution* (1970).

3. Cf. Dittmer (1974).

4. *Zhongguo gongchandang zhongyang weiyuanhui guanyu jianguo yilai* (1981, pp. 22ff.); in German: *Beijing Rundschau* 27 (1981): 19ff.

5. Cf. Selections from *China Mainland Magazines* 645: 17.

6. Ibid.

7. Ibid.: 18.

8. Ibid.: 19. On this point see Dreyer (1976), pp. 205 ff. especially p. 209.

9. *Wengge Fengyun* 2 (1968), in *Survey of China Mainland Press* 3970: 1; op. cit. Dreyer (1976), p. 209.

10. Cf. *China aktuell*, October 1977: 694.

11. "Statute of the Ninth CPC Party Congress," cf. *Hongqi* 4 (1969); in German: *Beijing Rundschau* 18 (1969): 38ff.; "Statute of the Tenth Party Congress" in: *Dokumente des X. Parteitages der KP China* (1973): 137ff.; "Statute of the Eleventh Party Congress" in *Dokumente des XI. Parteitages der KP China* (1977, pp. 137ff.).

12. *Renmin ribao*, October 3, 1978; *New China News Agency*, January 29, 1978; *Sixiang zhanxian* 3 (1978): 5.

13. *Sixiang zhanxian* 3 (1978): 5.

14. Cf. *Zhongguo shaoshu minzu jianshuo* (1974), p. 14.

15. *Zhongyang minzu xueyuan xuebao* 4 (1980): 9.

16. *Minzu yanjiu* 6 (1980): 6–7.

17. *Renmin ribao*, October 20, 1978; *Minzu tuanjie* 2 (1979): 4.

18. *Renmin ribao*, July 14, 1981.

19. *Minzu yanjiu* 6 (1980): 6.

20. *Minzu tuanjie* 5 (1980): 2f.; *Minzu tuanjie* 2 (1980): 10.

21. *Guizhou minzu yanjiu* 1 (1981): 8.

22. *Renmin ribao*, October 20, 1978; *Minzu tuanjie* 5 (1980): 19.

23. *Minzu yanjiu* 3 (1980): 6.

24. *Minzu tuanjie* 3 (1980): 6; *Guizhou minzu yanjiu* 2 (1981): 15.

25. *Minzu gongzuo* 2 (1981): 15.

26. *Sixiang zhanxian* 3 (1978): 14.

27. Cf. also *Minzu yuwen* 2 (1980): 2; *Guizhou minzu yanjiu* 1 (1981): 4; *Zhongyang minzu xueyuan xuebao* 2 (1980): 42.

28. *Nei menggu shehui kexue* 2 (1980): 143.

29. *Renmin ribao*, December 9, 1978.

30. *Minzu tuanjie* 4 (1980): 23; *Minzu tuanjie* 5 (1980): 3.

31. *Renmin ribao*, October 3, 1978 and August 28, 1978.

32. *Minzu tuanjie* 4 (1980): 23; *Renmin ribao*, October 12, 1978.

33. *Minzu tuanjie* 4 (1980): 23; *Sixiang zhanxian* 3 (1978): 6.

34. *Minzu tuanjie* 1 (1980): 41ff.

35. *Minzu tuanjie* 8 (1980): 32ff.; *Sixiang zhanxian* 3 (1977): 71ff. On the assimilation policy during the Cultural Revolution also see *Nei menggu shehui kexue* 1 (1982): 8f.

36. *Renmin ribao*, November 21, 1980; in German: *Beijing Rundschau* 48 (190): 19.

37. Ibid.

38. *Minzu tuanjie* 2 (1979): 2–4; *Minzu tuanjie* 5 (1980): 22; *Renmin ribao*, October 20, 1978 and December 15, 1978.

39. *Minzu tuanjie* 2 (1980): 10.

40. *Minzu tuanjie* 4 (1980): 2.

41. *Minzu tuanjie* 2 (1980): 10.

42. *Beijing Rundschau* 4 (1975): 16.

Chapter 3

1. *Minzu yanjiu* 3 (1983): 80f.

2. See on this point Ya Hanzhang (1980); Yang Kun (1983), pp. 82ff.; Yang Kun (1984), pp. 188ff.

3. Stalin (1976), p. 272.

4. See Rogatshew et al. (1966). The debate is outlined in Oberländer (1968); Oberländer (1971), pp. 273ff.

5. Quoted in Brunner et al. (1982), p. 20.

6. See for example Wang Guodong (1982), p. 9.

7. See on this point *Zhongnan minzu Xueyuan xuebao* 4 (1985): 72ff.

8. Zhaonastu (1981); *Yuguzu jianshi* (1983), pp. 6ff.

9. See on this point Heberer (1982), pp. 14ff.

10. *Zhongguo shehui kexue* 1 (1980): 155.

11. Professor Lin Yaohua in a talk at the Central Nationality Institute on August 8, 1979.

12. *Guizhou minzu yanjiu* 3 (1981): 96.

13. Bauer (1924), p. 139.

14. *Guizhou minzu yanjiu* 4 (1981): 11ff.

15. *Yunnan shehui kexue* 3 (1982): 37; similarly, see the anthropologist Yang Kun (1984), p. 136.

16. *Minzu yanjiu* 3 (1984): 1ff.

17. See on this point *Yunnan shehui kexue* 2 (1984): 3.

18. Fei Xiaotong in *Zhongguo shehui kexue* 1 (1980): 148.

19. Ibid.: 150–152.

20. *Guizhou minzu yanjiu* 3 (1981): 96.

21. *Zhongguo shehui kexue* 1 (1980): 157f.

22. *Minzu wenhua* 4 (1983): 62f.

23. *Shijie zongjiao yanjiu* 4 (1984): 140ff.

24. *Zhongyang minzu xueyuan xuebao* 3 (1985): 97.

25. Ibid.

26. *Yunnan shehui kexue* 2 (1982): 45ff.; *China Reconstructs* 7 (1983): 14ff.; *Yunnan shaoshu minzu* (1983): 263ff.

27. *Zhongyang minzu xueyuan xuebao* 4 (1983): 44ff.

28. *Xinjiang daxue xuebao* 1 (1985): 41–49.

29. The Central Asian expert Rong Xingjiang of Beijing University in a talk with the author on June 3, 1985.

30. *Zhongguo jianshe* 1 (1985): 47.

31. On this point see the report by Opletal (1983).

32. On this point see *Minzu gongzuo shiyong fagui shouce* (1958), 187ff.
33. *Minzu tuanjie* 11 (1985): 24.

Chapter 4

1. *Zhongguo shaoshu minzu* 12 (1988): 25; *Minzu tuanjie* 2 (1989): 37.
2. See *Policy towards Nationalities of the People's Republic of China* (1953); *Minzu gongzuo shiyong fagui shouce* (1958).
3. *Constitution of the People's Republic of China* 10 (1954): 40–43.
4. *Renmin ribao*, September 5, 1980; *Renmin ribao*, September 10, 1980.
5. *Minzu tuanjie* 10 (1980): 4.
6. *Renmin ribao*, December 5, 1981; *Beijing Review* 52 (1982).
7. On this point see *Renmin ribao*, (December 12, 1982.
8. *Renmin ribao*, September 13, 1980; *Renmin ribao*, September 16, 1980; *Renmin ribao*, September 19, 1980.
9. *Minzu tuanjie* 6 (1984): 3ff.; in German: Heberer (1984a), pp. 601ff.
10. *Minzu tuanjie* 11 (1986): 1.
11. See *Xinjiang ribao*, August 4, 1988.
12. *Renmin ribao*, September 9, 1988.
13. *Guangxi shehui kexue* 3 (1988): 7f.
14. *Minzu tuanjie* 7 (1986): 4f.
15. *Renmin ribao*, December 5, 1981.
16. *Liangshan bao*, June 5, 1986.
17. On this point see *Zhongguo tongji nianjian* (1986), p. 82.
18. *Guangxi shehui kexue* 3 (1988): 7f.
19. *yanjiu tuanjie* 10 (1985): 48.
20. *Guizhou minzu yanjiu* 3 (1981): 70f.
21. On this point see "Statutes of the Communist Party of China" in *Beijing Review* 38 (1982).

Chapter 5

1. On Yunnan's ethnic minorities: *Yunnan gaikuang* (1980); *Xinan minzu yanjiu* (1983); *Yunnan shaoshu minzu* (1983); Song Enchang, (1986); *Yunnan minzu gaikuang huiji* 2 (1986).
2. *Yunnan shehui kexue* 5 (1982): 23; *Jingji wenti tansuo* 10 (1984): 3ff.
3. *Jingji yanjiu* 12 (1980): 52f.; *Renmin ribao*, January 9, 1984.
4. Xu Jingjun (1983), pp. 202ff.
5. *Yunnan shengqing* (1986), pp. 100ff.
6. *Yunnan minzu xueyuan xuebao* 3 (1984): 39ff.; *Minzu tuanjie* 2 (1985): 16f.
7. *Yunnan shehui kexue* 4 (1984): 6; *Jingji wenti tansuo* 7 (1984): 11ff.
8. *Jingji wenti tansuo* 5 (1987): 14.
9. *Jingji wenti tansuo* 4 (1984): 2.
10. *Jingji wenti tansuo* 6 (1984): 30.
11. *Renmin ribao*, August 8, 1983.
12. *Yunnan shehui kexue* 4 (1984): 6ff.; *Minzu yanjiu* 1 (1985): 66ff.
13. *Minzu yanjiu* 1(1985): 64ff.
14. *Yunnan shehui kexue* 6 (1984): 25ff.
15. Ibid, 30; *Jingji wenti tansuo* 5 (1984): 37ff.
16. *Yunnan shehui kexue* 2 (1985): 71ff.

17. *Renmin ribao*, August 6, 1984; *Yunnan shehui kexue* 4 (1984): 11ff.; *Yunnan shehui kexue* 6 (1986): 28f.

18. *Yunnan shehui kexue* 6 (1984): 27ff.

19. On this point see *Jingji wenti tansuo* 1 (1983): 19f.; *Jingji wenti tansuo* 1 (1985): 14ff.

20. See *Jingji wenti tansuo* 10 (1984): 4ff.; *Yunnan duo minzu tese de shehuizhuyi xiandaihua wenti yanjiu* (1986), pp. 1ff.

21. *Jingji wenti tansuo* 11 (1984): 17ff.; *Yunnan ribao*, May 20, 1986.

22. Five-year plan in *Beijing Review* 17 (1986).

23. *Jingji wenti tansuo* 8 (1984): 42ff.; *Jingji wenti tansuo* 1 (1983): 19f.

24. Xu Jingjun (1983), p. 1f.

25. *Minzu tuanjie* 6 (1982): 19ff.; *Yunnan shehui kexue* 3 (1983): 23ff.

26. *Jingji wenti tansuo* 3 (1983): 30ff.; *Jingji wenti tansuo* 10 (1983): 41ff.; *Minzu tuanjie* 2 (1983): 21f.

27. *Jingji wenti tansuo* 10 (1984); *Yunnan shehui kexue* 5 (1984): 1ff.; *Yunnan zizhi difang jiajie* (1985), 2ff.

28. *Jingji wenti tansuo* 4 (1983): 30ff.; *Yunnan shehui kexue* 3 (1983): 31ff. On this point see also *Yunnan minzu jingji wenti jianghua* (1984), pp. 1ff.

29. *Jingji wenti tansuo* 8 (1984): 42ff.

30. Ibid.; *Minzu gongzuo* 1 (1985): 15ff.

31. *Jingji wenti tansuo* 7 (1987): 12.

Chapter 6

1. *Zhongguo 1982 nian renkou pucha ziliao* (1985), p. 16.

2. *Renmin ribao*, July 9, 1987.

3. *Zhongguo Jihua Shengyu Bao*, August 14, 1987.

4. Cf. *Jingji yanjiu* 3 (1979): 55ff.; *Jingji yanjiu* 8 (1979): 17ff.; *Jingji yanjiu* 12 (1981): 32ff.

5. Liao Tianping et al. (1982), pp. 127ff.; Yang Deqing (1983), pp. 13ff.; Tian Xueyuan (1984), pp. 1ff.

6. *Guangming ribao*, March 19, 1987; *Renkou yu sichua* (1981), p. 373. Worldwide, the per capita cultivated area is 0.5 ha.

7. *Shehui* 1 (1983): 57.

8. Compare *Zhongguo shehui kexue* 6 (1985): 36.

9. *Renmin ribao*, May 14, 1988.

10. *China Daily*, July 1, 1987.

11. *Jiankang bao*, October 29, 1988.

12. On the population question see Liu Zheng et al. (1981); *Chinese Sociology and Anthropology* 3-4 (1984); Hsu Mei Ling (1985), pp. 214ff.

13. *Renmin ribao*, September 16, 1982.

14. *Zhongyang minzu xueyuan xuebao* 2 (1982): 34.

15. *Renkou yanjiu* 1 (1981): 15.

16. Ibid.: 14–16.

17. *Nei menggu daxue Xxebao* 3 (1981): 19ff; *Renkou yanjiu* 2 (1981): 35f.; similarly: *Xibei renkou* 1 (1983). The periodical *Xibei renkou* 2 (1980) reports the same on the Gangca and Zekog cantons (autonomous district Haibai inhabited by Tibetans and the autonomous district of Huangnan of the Tibetans) in the province of Qinghai.

18. *Zhongguo minzu xueyuan xuebao* 2 (1982): 35.

19. The minister Chen Muhua at that time responsible for family planing quoted in *Guangming ribao*, October 27, 1981.
20. *Zhongyang minzu xueyuan xuebao* 2 (1982): 55.
21. Ibid.: 37.
22. *Beijing Review* 3 (1984): 20.
23. See *Xinan minzu xueyuan xuebao* 3 (1985): 122.
24. *Renkou yanjiu* 1 (1987): 20.
25. *Beijing Review* 33 (1987).
26. Information from the district family planing office in Xichang.
27. *Hulun Buir meng qi* (1986), p. 12.
28. *Qinghai minzu renkou wenti tantao* (1984), p. 12.
29. Ibid.
30. *Renkou yanjiu* 1 (1987): 37.
31. *Renmin ribao*, May 3, 1987.
32. Ibid.: 38.
33. *China Daily*, May 6, 1986.
34. *Zhongguo shaoshu minzu* 12 (1985): 101.
35. *Guizou shehui kexue* 5 (1987): 21.
36. *Zhongguo shehui kexue* 1 (1986): 80.
37. *Renkou yanjiu* 1 (1987): 38.
38. Among the Moslem minorities in the countryside in Xinjiang, girls usually marry between 15 and 16 and boys at 16 or 17. Since the legal age of marriage is considerably higher, the marriages either are not officially recorded or false ages are given; see *Renkou yanjiu* 1 (1987): 38.
39. *Zhongguo shehui kexue* 5 (1986): 50.
40. *Beijing Review* 48 (1986): 19.
41. *Zhongguo shehui kexue* 1 (1986): 84f.; *Renkou yanjiu* 4 (1987): 41f.
42. *Zhongguo renmin gongheguo laonian renkou dituji* (1986), p. 11/3.
43. Cf. *Renkou yanjiu* 4 (1987): 41f.
44. Ibid.: 42.
45. *China News Analysis* 720 (1986).
46. Tien Hung-mao (1974).
47. Cf. Orleans (1972), p. 89.
48. See for example, *China News Analysis*, nos. 1052, 1076; *China aktuell* 12 (1975): 758.
49. Du Wenzhen (1985), p. 109.
50. *Renkou yu jingji* 2 (1987): 3f.
51. Tian Fang and Lin Fatang (1986), p. 292.
52. Tian Fang and Lin Fatang (1986), pp. 286ff.
53. On this point see *Eine grosse Schule für Chinas Jugend* (1976).
54. *Minzu gongzuo* (1981): 8.
55. See *Jingji yanjiu* 4 (1983): 53ff.; Weggel (1984), 110ff.; *Jiankang bao*, December 12, 1986; Si Ping (1986), p. 35f.
56. *Qinghai minzu renkou wenti tantao* (1984), p. 29; *Zhongguo tongji nianjian* (1986).
57. *Minzu yanjiu* 4 (1985): 3.
58. *Jingji ribao*, April 7, 1984.
59. On the tensions in Xinjiang see *Zhengming* 43 (1981): 24. Uprisings were reported in Inner Mongolia in October 1981 after the decision of the central government to settle another 400,000 Han Chinese there. See *China aktuell* 12 (1981): 785.

Renmin ribao indirectly confirmed the unrest in Inner Mongolia in an appeal to strengthen unity among the nationalities. Such an appeal generally follows conflicts between Han and ethnic minorities in a region; on this point see also *Nei menggu shehui kexue* 1 (1982): 9.

60. For example Hu Huanyong et al., vol. 3 (1985): 21ff.
61. *Zhongguo shehui kexue* 4 (1981): 44.
62. *Minzu tuanjie* 7 (1985): 10.
63. *Nei menggu shehui kexue* 4 (1984): 19f.
64. *Jingji yanjiu* 3 (1984): 58; *Renkou yanjiu* 6 (1984): 57; Tian Fang and Lin Fatang (1986), pp. 106ff., 194.
65. *Jingji ribao*, April 4, 1984.
66. The population increased by 31 percent between 1970 and 1980, while livestock increased by only 27 percent, and pasturelands decreased in area; see *Minzu yanjiu* 4 (1985): 3.

Chapter 7

1. On this point see: Israeli (1980); Bai Shouyi (1982); *Yisilanjiao zai Zhongguo* (1982); *Zhongguo Yisilanjiao shi cankao ziliao* 2 (1985).
2. Peng Yingquan (1983); Song Enchang (1985); Seiwert (1987).
3. See de Groot (1910); Grube (1910); Weber (1920); E. R. and K. Hughes (1950); Maspero (1950); Granet (1951); Yang (1961); Thompson (1969); Eichhorn (1973); Heberer (1988a), pp. 41ff.; idem. (1988b).
4. Lin Yutang (1947), p. 136f.
5. Wilhelm (1983), pp. 270ff.
6. See Bush (1970), Chan Wing-tsit (1953).
7. *Fundamental Laws of the Chinese Soviet Republic* (1934), p. 22.
8. Mao Zedong (1968), p. 48.
9. Zhou Enlai (1984), p. 388f.
10. *Renmin ribao*, August 8, 1963; see also MacInnis (1974).
11. *Minzu tuanjie* 1 (1980): 40.
12. *Renmin ribao*, October 20, 1978; *Minzu tuanjie* 3 (1980): 16.
13. On this point see *Minzu tuanjie* 2 (1980): 12f; *Minzu tuanjie* 6 (1981): 10. On the destruction in Tibet see also Lehmann and Ullal (1981), pp. 50ff.
14. *Beijing Review* 52 (1982): 14.
15. *Constitution of the People's Republic of China* (1954).
16. *Beijing Review* 11 (1978): 14.
17. *Renmin ribao*, July 7, 1979; in German: *China aktuell* 7 (1979): 822.
18. *Renmin ribao*, March 15, 1979; *Ningxia ribao*, November 12, 1981; *Yunnan ribao*, December 18, 1981.
19. Bauer (1984), p. 5.
20. Ibid., p. 6.
21. *Guangming ribao*, November 11, 1980; *Qinghai ribao*, August 30, 1981; *Guangming ribao*, June 27, 1982.
22. *Minzu tuanjie* 12 (1980): 30f.
23. *Renmin ribao*, August 22, 1987.
24. *Renmin ribao*, April 26, 1986; *China Daily*, April 4, 1987; *Renmin ribao*, August 22, 1987.
25. *Gongren ribao*, February 2, 1987.
26. *Guangming ribao*, June 12, 1986.

27. *Shijie Zongjiao yanjiu* 1 (1986): 143ff; *Xueshu jikan* 3 (1986): 12ff; *Guizhou minzu yanjiu* 2 (1987): 151ff; *Ningxia shehui kexue* 3 (1987): 66; *Ningxia shehui kexue* 5 (1987): 81ff; *Sixiang zhanxian* 2 (1987): 12f.; *Zhongguo shehui kexue* 4 (1987): 36ff.
28. *Renmin ribao*, November, 11, 1985.
29. *Renmin ribao*, May 31, 1982.
30. Ibid.
31. *Xizang ribao*, February 2, 1982; *Renmin ribao*, March 19, 1982.
32. *Hongqi* 12 (1982): 3.
33. *Zhongyang minzu xueyuan xuebao* 3 (1982): 17.
34. Interview in *Das neue China* 6 (1982): 7.

Chapter 8

1. Li Tieh-Tsang (1956); International Commission of Jurists (1959, 1960); Dalai Lama (1962); Tomson (1963), pp. 42ff.; Ginsburgs and Mathos (1964); Richardson (1964); Shakabpa (1967); Rubin (1968); Tomson and Su (1972), pp. 224ff.; Norbu (1974); Burman (1979); Gyaltsen (1979); Norbu (1979); Weyer (1982); Epstein (1983); Wersto (1983); Wang Furen; Suo Wenqing (1984); *Tibet: Gestern und Heute* (1984); Richardson (1985); Norbu (1987); *Tibet: Traum oder Trauma?* (1987); Van Walts Van Praag (1987); Kelly and Bastian (1988).
2. See *Far Eastern Economic Review*, October 13, 1988, 26.
3. On this question see Bell (1924); Filchner (1942); Leifer (1959), pp. 42ff.; Burman (1979), Wang Furen and Su Wenting (1981), pp. 124ff., 137; Zhou Weizhou (1984).
4. See also Tomson (1963), p. 42.
5. Ross (1942), p. 255.
6. Filchner (1942), p. VIf.
7. On the Tibet question see also Rubin (1968), pp. 110ff.; Weggel (1984).
8. Cited in Arecaga (1982), p. 19.
9. Ibid.
10. Ibid., p. 20.
11. Compare Wang Tieya (1981), pp. 60ff.
12. On this destruction see Lehmann and Ullal (1981).
13. *Beijing Review* (German edition) 41 (1988): 7f.

Chapter 9

1. Wang Enmao (1988), 3ff.

Glossary

Nationality	Chinese
Achang	阿昌族
Bai	白族
Bulang	布朗族
Bonan	保安族
Bouyei	布依族
Dai	傣族
Daur	达斡尔族
Deang (originally Benglong)	德昂族 (崩龙)
Drung	独龙族
Dong	侗族
Dongxiang	东乡族
Ewenki	鄂温克族
Gaoshan	高山族
Gelo	仡佬族
Hani	哈尼族
Hezhen	赫哲族
Hui	回族

Nationality	Chinese
Jingpo	景颇族
Jinuo	基诺族
Kazak	哈萨克族
Kirgiz	柯尔克孜族
Korean	朝鲜族
Lahu	拉祜族
Lhoba	珞巴族
Li	黎族
Lisu	傈僳族
Manchu	满族
Maonan	毛难族
Miao	苗族
Moinba	门巴族
Mongolian	蒙古族
Mulam	仫佬族
Naxi	纳西族
Nu	怒族
Oroqen	鄂伦春族
Pumi	普米族
Qiang	羌族
Russian	俄罗斯族
Salar	撒拉族
She	畲族
Shui	水族
Tajik	塔吉克族
Tatar	塔塔尔族
Tibetan	藏族
Tu	土族
Tujia	土家族
Uzbek	乌孜别克族
Uygur	维吾尔族

Nationality	Chinese
Va	佤族
Xibe	锡伯族
Yao	瑶族
Yi	彝族
Yugur	裕固族
Zhuang	壮族

Bibliography

Allworth, Edward, ed. 1971. *Soviet Nationality Problems*. New York, London: Columbia University Press.

Arecaga, J. De. 1982. "Die Internationale Gemeinschaft und das Prinzip der Selbstbestimmung der Völker." *Internationale Politik* 768.

Azrael, Jeremy R., ed. 1958. *Soviet Nationality Policies and Practices*. New York: Praeger.

Bai Shouyi. 1981. "Guanyu Zhongguo minzu guanxi shi shangde jige wenti" (Some questions on nationalities' relations in history). *Beijing Shifan Daxue Xuebao* 6.

———. 1982. *Zhongguo Yisilanjiao shi cungao* (Materials on the history of Islam in China). Yinchuan: Ningxia renmin chubanshe.

Bauer, Otto. 1924. *Die Nationalitätenfrage und die Sozialdemokratie*. Vienna: Wiener Volksbuchhandlung.

Bauer, Wolfgang, ed. 1980. *China und die Fremden*. Munich: Beck.

Bell, Charles. 1924. *Tibet, Past and Present*. Oxford: Clarendon Press.

Beschluss des ZK des KPCh über die Grosse Proletarische Kulturrevolution. 1966. Beijing: Verlag für Fremdsprachige Literatur.

Biegert, Claus. 1981. *Seit 200 Jahren ohne Verfassung. USA: Indianer im Widerstand*. Reinbek: Rowohlt.

Brunner, Georg and Boris Meissner. 1982. *Nationalitätenprobleme in der Sowjetunion und Osteuropa*. Cologne: Markus.

Burman, Bina Roy. 1979. *Religion and Politics in Tibet*. New Delhi: Vikas.

Bush, R. C. 1970. *Religion in Communist China*. New York: Abingdon.

Chaliand, Gerard, ed. 1980. *People Without a Country: The Kurds and Kurdistan*. London: World Minorities.

Chan Wing-tsit. 1953. *Religious Trends in Modern China*. New York: Columbia University Press.

Chen, Jack. 1977. *The Sinkiang Story*. New York: Macmillan.

Chiang Kai-shek. 1947. *China's Destiny*. New York: Macmillan.

Chiang Kai-shek and May Ling. 1945. *Unser China*. Zürich: Rascher.

China Handbook 1937–1945. 1947. New York: Macmillan.

Constitution of the People's Republic of China. 1954. Beijing: Foreign Languages Press.

Dalai Lama. 1962. *Mein Leben und mein Volk. Die Tragödie Tibets.* Munich.
de Groot, J. J. M. 1910. *The Religious System of China.* 6 vols. Leyden: Brill.
d'Encausse, Helene C. 1979. *Risse im Roten Imperium. Das Nationalitätenproblem in der Sowjetunion.* Vienna, Munich: Molden.
Ding Wang. 1967. *Wenhua da geming pinglun ji* (Discussion material about the Cultural Revolution). Hong Kong: n. p.
Dittmer, Lowell. 1974. *Liu Shao-ch'i and the Chinese Cultural Revolution. The Politics of Mass Criticism.* Berkeley, Los Angeles, and London: University of California Press.
Dokumente des X Parteitages der KP China. 1973. Beijing: Verlag für Fremdsprachige Literatur.
Dokumente des XI Parteitages der KP China. 1977. Beijing: Verlag für Fremdsprachige Literatur.
Dreyer, June T. 1976. *China's Forty Millions.* Cambridge, Mass. and London: Harvard University Press.
Du Wenzhen. 1985. *Renkou zongheng tan* (On the population). Beijing: Zhongguo qingnian chubanshe.
Eberhard, Wolfram. 1942. *Kultur und Siedlung der Randvölker Chinas.* Supplement to vol. 36. Leiden: T'oung Pao.
Eichhorn, W. 1973. *Die Religionen Chinas.* Stuttgart: Kohlhammer.
Eine grosse Schule für Chinas Jugend—ihr Leben auf dem Land. 1976. Beijing: Verlag für Fremdsprachige Literatur.
Epstein, Israel. 1983. *Tibet Transformed.* Beijing: New World Press.
Filchner, Wilhelm. 1942. *Sturm über Asien.* Berlin.
Fleischmann, Klaus. 1976. *Die neue Verfassung der Union von Birma. Vorgeschichte, Inhalte, Wirklichkeit.* Hamburg: Institut für Asienkunde.
Francis, Emerich. 1965. *Ethnos und Demos.* Berlin: Duncker und Humblot.
Franke, Otto. 1967. *Geschichte des Chinesischen Reiches*, vol. 1. Reprint. Taipei: n. p.
Fremery, Michael. 1983. "Indonesien." In Nohlen, Dieter and Franz Nuscheler, eds. *Handbuch der Dritten Welt 7.* Hamburg: Hoffmann und Campe.
Fundamental Laws of the Chinese Soviet Republic. With an Introduction by Bela Kun. 1934. London: n. p.
Gesellschaft für Bedrohte Völker, Arbeitsgruppe Indianer, ed. 1982. "Der Völkermord geht weiter." Reinbek: Rowohlt.
Ginsburgs, George and Michael Mathos. 1964. *Communist China and Tibet.* The Hague: Martinus Nijhoff.
Granet, Marcel. 1951. *La Religion des Chinois.* Paris: Presses Universitaires de France.
Grube, Wilhelm. 1910. *Religion und Kultus der Chinesen.* Leipzig: Haupt.
Gyaltsen, Gyaltag. 1979. *Tibet einst und heute.* Rikon: The Office of Tibet.
Han Suyin. 1978. *Chinas Sonne über Lhasa.* Bern and Munich: Scherz.
Heberer, Thomas. 1982. "Die sprachenpolitik gegenüber den nationalen Minderheiten in China." *Sprache und Herrschaft* 11.
————. 1984a. "Das Gesetz über die Gebietsautonomie der Nationalitäten der VR China." Translation and commentary in *China aktuell* (October).
————. 1984b. "Nationalitätenpolitik und Entwicklungspolitik in den Gebieten nationaler Minderheiten in China." *Bremer Beiträge zur Geographie und Raumplanung.* Bremen: University Press.
————. 1985. "Kulturwandel der Minderheiten in der VR China am Beispiel der

Sitten und Gebräuche der Yi." *Minoritas* 1.

————. 1987, ed. *Ethnic Minorities in China: Tradition and Transformation. Papers of the 2nd Interdisciplinary Congress Sinology/Ethnology St. Augustin.* Aachen: Edition Herodot.

————. 1988a. *Wenn der Drache sich erhebt. China zwischen Gestern und Heute.* Baden-Baden: Signal.

————. 1988b. "Opium des Volkes? China Religionsfreiheit im Lichte der Tradition." In Steckel and Helmut, eds. *China im widerspruch. Mit Konfuzius ins 21. Jahrhundert?* Reinbek: Rowohlt.

Heidhues, Mary F. 1983. *Politik in Südostasien.* Hamburg: Institut für Asienkunde.

Hero, Dilip. 1977. "The Adivaris: The 'Scheduled' Tribes of India." In Asworth, G. 1977. London: World Minorities.

Hosie, A. 1972. *Three Years in Western China.* Reprint. Taipei: n. p.

Hsu Mei Ling. 1985. "Growth and Control of Population in China: The Urban-Rural Contrast." *Annals of the Association of American Geographers* 2.

Hsü, L. Shilien, ed. 1933. *Sun Yat-sen: His Political and Social Ideas.* Los Angeles: University of Southern California Press.

Hu Huanyong et al., eds. 1985. *Renkou yanjiu lunwenji* (Collection of essays on population research). 3 vols. Shanghai: Huadong shifan daxue chubanshe.

Hughes, E. R. and Hughes, K. 1950. *Religion in China.* London: Hutchinson.

Hulun Buir meng qi (Description of the situation in the Hulun-Buir League). 1986. Hohhot: Nei menggu renmin chubanshe.

International Commission of Jurists. 1959. "The Question of Tibet and the Rule of Law." Geneva: International Commission of Jurists.

————. 1960. "Tibet and the Chinese People's Republic." Geneva: International Commission of Jurists.

Israeli, Raphael. 1980. *Muslims in China.* London and Malmö: Curzon and Humanities Press.

Kelly, Petra and Bastian Gert, eds. 1988. *Tibet—ein vergewaltigtes Land.* Reinbek: Rowohlt.

Krag, Helen L. 1983. *Die Sowjetunion—Staat, Nationalitätenfrage und Sprachenpolitik.* Vienna: Sprache und Herrschaft.

Kunstadter, Peter, ed. 1976. *Southeast Asian Tribes, Minorities and Nations.* 2 vols. Princeton: University Press.

Kurzrock, R., ed. 1974. *Minderheiten.* Berlin: Colloquium.

Lattimore, Owen. 1962. *Inner Asian Frontiers of China.* Boston: Little, Brown.

Lehmann, Peter-Hannes and Jay Ullal. 1981. *Tibet—Das stille Drama auf dem Dach der Erde.* Hamburg: Geo.

Leifer, Walter. 1959. *Weltenprobleme am Himalaya.* Würtzburg: Marienburg.

Li Gi. 1981. *Das Buch der Riten, Sitten und Gebräuche.* Ed. R. Wilhelm. Cologne and Düsseldorf: Diederichs.

Li Tieh-Tsang. 1956. *The Historical Status of Tibet.* New York: n. p.

Liao Tianping and Wen Yingqian. 1982. *Liangzhong shengchan lilun he wo guo de renkou wenti* (The theory of two types of production and the population question of our country). Guangzhou: Guangzhou renmin chubanshe.

Lin Yutang. 1947. *Mein Land und mein Volk.* Stuttgart: Deutsche Verlagsanstalt.

Liu Qinbin. 1981. "Lun Sun Zhongshan minzuzhuyi sixiang" (On the nationalist ideas of Sun Yat-sen). *Ningxia Daxue Xuebao* 4.

Liu Zheng, Song Jian, and others. 1981. *China's Population. Problems and Prospects.* Beijing: New World Press.

Louis, Victor. 1977. *The Coming Decline of the Chinese Empire*. New York: Times Books.

MacInnis, D. E. 1974. *Religionspolitik im Kommunistischen China*. Göttingen: Vandenhoeck and Ruprecht.

Mao Zedong. 1968. *Ausgewählte Werke*, vol. 1. Beijing: Verlag für Fremdsprachige Literatur.

Maspero, H. 1950. *Les Religions Chinoises*. Paris: Civilisations du Sud.

Minzu gongzuo shiyong fagui shouce (Handbook on legal regulations for nationality work). 1958. Beijing: Gongren chubanshe.

Minzu yuwen lunji (Treatises of the languages of the nationalities). 1981. Beijing: Zhongguo shehui chubanshe.

Minzu yuwen yanjiu (Studies on the nationalities' languages). 1983. Chengdu: Sichuan minzu chubanshe.

Minzu yuwen yanjiu wenji (Collection on studies on nationalities' written languages). 1982. Xining: Qinghai minzu chubanshe.

Morrock, R. 1972. "Minority Nationalities in China." *Journal of Contemporary Asia* 2.

Münzel, Mark, ed. 1981. *Die indianische Verweigerung. Lateinamerikas Ureinwohner zwischen Ausrottung und Selbstbestimmung*. Reinbek: Rowohlt.

Nairn, Tom et al. 1977. *Nationalismus und Marxismus*. Berlin: Rotbuch.

"Nationalitätenfragen in der UdSSR, Polen und Jugoslawien." 1971. *Osteuropa* 1.

Norbu, Dawa. 1974. *Red Star over Tibet*. London: Collins.

—————. 1979. "The 1959 Tibetan Rebellion: An Interpretation." *The China Quarterly* 77.

—————. 1987. "The Future of Taiwan in the Tibetan Model." *China Report* 23.

Oberländer, E. 1968. "Der sowjetische Nationsbegriff." *Aus Politik und Zeitgeschichte* 12.

—————. 1971. "Der sowjetische Nationsbegriff heute." *Osteuropa* 4.

Opletal, Helmut. 1983. "Die letzten Juden von Kaifeng." *Frankfurter Rundschau* (July 23).

Orleans, L. A. 1972. *Every Fifth Child: The Population of China*. Stanford: Stanford University Press.

Peng Yingquan, ed. 1983. *Xizang zongjiao gaishuo* (The religions of Tibet). Lhasa: Xizang renmin chubanshe.

Pimenoff, Veronica. 1973. Marginale Minderheiten und phuralistische Ideologie. Dissertation: Hamburg.

Policy towards Nationalities of the People's Republic of China. 1953. Beijing: Foreign Languages Press.

Qinghai minzu renkou wenti tantao (Debate on the population problem of nationalities in Qinghai). 1984. Xining: Qinghai renmin chubanshe.

Razon, F. and R. Hensman. 1976. *The Oppression of the Indigenous Peoples of the Philippines*. Copenhagen: International Work Group for Indigenous Affairs.

Renkou yu sichua (Population and the Four Modernizations). 1981. Dukou: Sichuan renmin chubanshe.

Revesz, Laszlo. 1979. *Volk aus 100 Nationalitäten*. Bern: SOI.

Richardson, Hugh E. 1964. *Tibet—Geschichte und Schicksal*. Frankfurt and Berlin: Netzner.

—————. 1985. *Tibet and Its History*. London: Weidenfeld and Nicolson.

Roberts, Janine. 1979. *Nach Völkermord: Landraub und Uranabbau—Die Schwarzaustralier (Aborigines) kämpfen ums "Überleben."* Göttingen: Pogrom.

Rogatshew, M. and M. A. Swerdlin. 1966. "Über den Begriff der Nation." *Sowjetwissenschaft, Gesellschaftswissenschaftliche Beiträge* 6.

Ross, Colin. 1942. *Das Neue Asien*. Leipzig: Brockhaus.

Rubin, A. P. 1968. "The Position of Tibet in International Law." *The China Quarterly* 35.

Sao Saimong Mangrai. 1965. *The Shan States and the British Annexation*. Ithaca: n. p.

Scharping, T. 1981. *Umsiedlungsprogramme für Chinas Jugend 1955-1980*. Hamburg: Institut für Asienkunde.

Schickel, Joachim, ed. 1969. *Mao Tse-tung. Der Grosse Strategische Plan. Dokumente zur Kulturrevolution*. Hamburg: Voltaire.

Schild, Ilse. 1981. "Odyssee einer Roma-Gruppe in den Niederlanden." *Pogrom* 80/81.

Seiwert, Hubert. 1987. "On the Religions of National Minorities in the Context of China's Religious History." In Heberer (1987).

Shakabpa, T. W. D. 1967. *Tibet. A Political History*. New Haven: Yale University Press.

Si Ping, ed. 1986. *Kaifa bianqu yu sanli zhibian*. Hohhot: Nei menggu renmin chubanshe.

Song Enchang. 1985. *Zhongguo shaoshu minzu zongjiao* (Religions of the national minorities in China). Kunming: Yunnan renmin chubanshe.

————. 1986. *Yunnan shaoshu minzu yanjiu wenji* (Collected articles about the research of Yunnan's national minorities). Kunming: Yunnan renmin chubanshe.

Stalin, J. W. 1976. *Werke*, vol. 2. Dortmund: Roter Morgen.

Sun Yat-sen. 1927. *Die Grundlehren von dem Volkstum*. Berlin: Schlieffen.

————. 1953. *Memoirs of a Chinese Revolutionary*. Taipei: China Cultural Service.

Taiping Tianguo geming shiji, Guangxi nongmin qiyi ziliao (The revolutionary period of the heavenly Taiping Empire—material on the peasant uprisings in Guangxi). 1978. 2 vols. Beijing: Zhonghua Shuju.

Theodorson, G. A. 1964. "Minority peoples in the Union of Burma." *Journal of Southeast Asian History* 1.

Thompson, L. G. 1969. *Chinese Religion: An Introduction*. Belmont: Dickenson.

Tian Fang and Lin Fatang. 1986. *Zhongguo renkou qianyi* (China's population migration). Beijing: Zhishi chubanshe.

Tian Xueyuan. 1983. *Xin shiqi renkou lun* (On the population in the new period). Harbin: Heilongjiang renmin chubanshe.

————. 1984. *Zhongguo renkou kongzhi he fazhan yueshi yanjiu* (Studies on population control and trends in China). Beijing: Jingji kexue chubanshe.

Tibet: Gestern und Heute. 1984. Beijing: Beijing Rundschau.

Tibet: Traum oder Trauma? 1987. Göttingen: Pogrom.

Tien Hung-mao. 1974. "Sinicization of National Minorities in China." *Current Scene* 11.

Tomson, Edgar. 1963. *Die Volksrepublik China und das Recht Nationaler Minderheiten*. Frankfurt and Berlin: Metzner.

Tomson, Edgar and Su Jyun-Hsyong. 1972. *Regierung und Verwaltung der VR China*. Cologne: Verlag Wissenschaft und Politik.

Van Walts Van Praag, Michael. 1987, *The Status of Tibet. History, Rights and Prospects in International Law*. Boulder: Westview.

Wang Enmao. 1988. "Weihu zuguo tongyi, zengqiang minzu tuanjie" (Safeguard the unity of the motherland, strengthen the unity of the nationalities). In *Shishi Qiushi* (Seek truth from facts) 5 (1988).

Wang Furen and Suo Wenqing. 1981. *Zangzu shiyao* (On the history of the Tibetans). Chengdu: Sichuan minzu chubanshe.

————. 1984. *Highlights of Tibetan History*. Beijing: New World Press.

Wang Guodong. 1982. *Minzu wenti changshi* (Elementary knowledge on the nationality question). Yinchuan: Ningxia renmin chubanshe.

Wang Shuwu. 1981. *Yunnan gu yishu chao* (Lost ancient writings from Yunnan). Kunming: Yunnan renmin chubanshe.

Wang Tieya, ed. 1981. *Guoji fa* (International law). Beijing: Fallü chubanshe.

Weber, Max. 1920. "Konfuzianismus und Taoismus." *Gesammelte Aufsätze zur Religionssoziologie*, vol. 1. Tübingen: Mohr.

Weggel, Oskar. 1984. *Xinjiang. Das Zentralasiatische China*. Hamburg: Intitut Für Asienkunde.

————. 1988. "Tibet von der Eigenständigkeit zur 'Befreiung.' Die drei Argumente Beijings." *Vereinte Nationen* 2 (1988).

Weng Dujian, ed. 1984. *Zhongguo minzu guanxi shi yanjiu* (Studies on the history of nationality relations in China). Beijing: Zhongguo shehui kexue chubanshe.

Wentzel, Sondra. 1985. *Schutz und Unterstützung ethnischer Minderheiten*. Gelsenkirchen: Andreas Müller.

Wersto, T. J. 1983. "Tibet in Sino-Soviet Relations." *Asian Affairs*, Fall.

West-Papua: The Obliteration of a People. 1983. London: Tapol.

Weyer, H. 1982. *Tibet—Wahrheit und Legende*. Karlsruhe.

Wichtige Dokumente der Grossen Proletarischen Kulturrevolution. 1970. Beijing: Verlag für Fremdsprachige Literatur.

Willoughby, Westel. 1920. *Foreign Rights and Interests in China*. Baltimore: n. p.

Wirth, Louis. 1945. "The Problem of Minority Groups." In Linton, R., ed. *The Science of Man in World Crisis*. New York: Columbia University Press.

Xinan minzu yanjiu (Studies on southwestern China's nationalities). 1983. Dukou: Sichuan minzu chubanshe.

Xinjiang jianshi (Short history of Xinjiang), vol. 2. 1980. Urümqi: Xinjiang renmin chubanshe.

Xu Jingjun. 1983. *Shanqu jingji* (Economy of the mountain regions). Kunming: Yunnan renmin chubanshe.

Ya Hanzhang. 1980. *Minzu xingcheng wenti yanjiu* (Research on the problem of the formation of nationalities). Zigong: Sichuan renmin chubanshe.

Yang, C. K. 1961. *Religion in Chinese Society*. Los Angeles: University of California Press.

Yang Deqing, ed. 1983. *Renkouxue gailun* (Introduction to population science). Shijiazhuang: Hubei renmin chubanshe.

Yang Kun. 1983. *Minzu yu minzuxue* (Nationality and ethnology). Dukou: Sichhuan minzu chubanshe.

————. 1984. *Minzuxue gailun* (Introduction to ethnology). Beijing: Zhongguo shehui kexue chubanshe.

Yisilanjiao zai Zhongguo (Islam in China). 1982. Yinchuan: Ningxia renmin chubanshe.

Yuguzu jianshi (Short history of the Yugur). 1983. Tianshui: Gansu minzu chubanshe.

Yunnan duo minzu tese de shehuizhuyi xiandaihua wenti yanjiu (Studies on the socialist modernization of Yunnan with distinctive multinationality features). 1986. Kunming: Yunnan renmin chubanshe.

Yunnan gaikuang (The situation in Yunnan). 1980. Kunming: Yunnan renmin chubanshe.

Yunnan minzu gaikuang huiji (Collection on the situation of nationalities in Yunnan), vol. 2. 1986. Kunming: Yunnan renmin chubanshe.

Yunnan minzu jingji wenti jianghua (Talks on the problems of Yunnan's multinationality economy). 1984. Kunming: Yunnan renmin chubanshe.

Yunnan shaoshu minzu (Yunnan's minorities). 1983. Kunming: Yunnan minzu chubanshe.

Yunnan shengqing 1949–1984 (The situation of Yunnan province). 1986. Kunming: Yunnan renmin chubanshe.

Yunnan tongji nianjian (Yunnan statistical yearbook). 1987. Kunming: Yunnan renmin chubanshe.

Yunnan Xinhai geming ziliao (Material on the Xianhai revolution in Yunnan). 1981. Kunming: Yunnan renmin chubanshe.

Yunnan zizhi difang jiajie (Brief characterization of the autonomous regions in Yunnan). 1985. Kunming: Yunnan renmin chubanshe.

Zhaonastu. 1981. *Dongbu Yuguyu jianzhi* (Introduction to the Eastern Yugur language). Beijing: Minzu chubanshe.

Zhongguo gongchandang zhongyang weiyuanhui guanyu jianguo yilai dangde ruogan lishi wenti de jueyi (Resolution on some questions in the history of the party since the founding of the People's Republic of China). 1981. Beijing: Renmin chubanshe.

Zhongguo jindaishi gao (China's modern history). 1978. Ed. The Research Institute for Modern Chinese History of the Chinese Academy of Social Sciences, vol. 1. Beijing: Renmin chubanshe.

Zhongguo jindaishi ziliao xuanbian (Selected material on the modern history of China), vol. 1. 1977. Ed. Department for Modern Chinese History of the Beijing Teachers Training College). Beijing: Zhonghua Shiju.

Zhongguo minzu guanxi shi lunwen xuanji (Collection of theses on the history of nationality relations in China). 1983. Lanzhou: Gansu minzu chubanshe.

Zhongguo minzu guanxi shi lunwenji (Collection of theses on the history of nationality relations in China). 1982. 2 vols. Beijing: Minzu chubanshe.

Zhongguo minzu yuwen lunwenji (Treatises on the languages of the nationalities of China). 1986. Chengdu: Sichuan minzu chubanshe.

Zhongguo 1982 nian renkou pucha ziliao (1982 population census of China). 1985. Beijing: Zhongguo tongji chubanshe.

Zhongguo renmin gongheguo laonian renkou dituji (Age atlas of the People's Republic of China). 1986. Beijing: Ditu chubanshe.

Zhongguo shaoshu minzu jianshuo (Short introduction of Chinese national minorities). 1974. 9 vols. Beijing: Minzu chubanshe.

Zhongguo shaoshu minzu yuyan (The languages of China's minorities). 1987. Chengdu: Sichuan minzu chubanshe.

Zhongguo tongji nianjian (Statistical yearbook of China). 1986. Beijing: Zhongguo tongji chubanshe.

————. 1987. Beijing: Zhongguo tongji chubanshe.

————. 1988. Beijing: Zhongguo tongji chubanshe.

Zhongguo Yisilanjiao shi cannkao ziliao (Materials on the history of Islam in China). 1985. 2 vols. Yinchuan: Ningxia renmin chubanshe.

Zhou Enlai. 1984. "Guanyu wo guo minzu zhengce de jige wenti" (A few questions on nationality policy in our country). *Zhou Enlai tongyi zhanxian wenxuan* (Selected articles of Zhou Enlai on the United Front). Beijing: Renmin chubanshe.

Zhou Liangxiao. 1981. "Lun Hubilie" (On Kublai Khan). *Zhongguo Shehui Kexue* 6.

Zhou Weizhou. 1984. *Ying-E qinlüe wo guo Xizang shi bei* (Historical strategy of England's and Russia's Encroachment in our Tibet). Xian: Shaanxi renmin chubanshe.

Periodicals, Newspapers

Asian Affairs
Asiaweek
Beijing Rundschau
Beijing shifan daxue xuebao (Journal of the Beijing Teachers Training College)
China aktuell
China Daily
China News Analysis
China Quarterly, The
China Reconstructs (German edition)
China Report
Chinese Sociology and Anthropology
Current Scene
Das neue China
Die Welt
Far Eastern Economic Review
Frankfurter Allgemeine
Frankfurter Rundschau
Geographische Rundschau
Gongren ribao (Workers Daily)
Guangming ribao (The Light)
Guangxi shehui kexue (Social Sciences of Guangxi)
Guizhou minzu yanjiu (Guizhou's Nationalities Studies)
Guizhou shehui kexue (Social Sciences of Guizhou)
Hongqi (Red Flag)
Internationale Politik
Jiankang bao (Health Newspaper)
Jingji ribao (Economic Daily)
Jingji wenti yansuo (Studies on Economic Problems)
Jingji yanjiu (Studies on Economics)
Journal of Contemporary Asia
Journal of Southeast Asian History
Liangshan bao (Liangshan Newspaper)
Lishi yanjiu (Historical Studies)
Minzu gongzuo (Nationalities Work)
Minzu tuanjie (Unity of the Nationalities)
Minzu wenhua (Nationalities Culture)
Minzu yanjiu (Nationalities Studies)
Minzu yuwen (Nationalities Languages)
Nei menggu daxue xuebao (Journal of the University of Inner Mongolia)
Nei menggu shehui kexue (Social Sciences of Inner Mongolia)
New China News Agency
Newsweek Magazine
Ningxia daxue xuebao (Journal of the Ningxia University)
Ningxia ribao (Ningxia Daily)

Ningxia shehui kexue (Social Sciences of Ningxia)
Osteuropa
Pogrom
Qinghai ribao (Qinghai Daily)
Qinghai shehui kexue (Social Sciences of Qinghai)
Renkou yanjiu (Population Studies)
Renkou yu jingji (Population and Economy)
Renmin ribao (People's Daily)
Selections from China Mainland Magazines
Shehui (Society)
Shijie zongjiao yanjiu (Studies on the World Religions)
Sixiang zhanxian (Ideological Front)
Survey of China Mainland Press
Xibei renkou (Population of the Northwest)
Xinan minzu xueyuan xuebao
        (Journal of the Nationalities Institute of the Southwest)
Xinjiang daxue xuebao (Journal of the Xinjiang University)
Xinjiang shehui kexue (Social Sciences of Xinjiang)
Xizang ribao (Tibet Daily)
Xizang yanjiu (Tibet Studies)
Xueshu jikan (Scientific Quarterly)
Yunnan minzu xueyuan xuebao (Journal of the Yunnan Nationalities Institute)
Yunnan ribao (Yunnan Daily)
Yunnan shehui kexue (Social Sciences of Yunnan)
Zhengming (Contend)
Zhongguo jianshe (China Reconstructs)
Zhongguo jihua shengyu cao (Chinese Family Planning Newspaper)
Zhongguo shaoshu minzu (China's National Minorities)
Zhongguo shehui kexue (China's Social Sciences)
Zhongguo shi yanjiu dongtai (Trends in China's Historical Research)
Zhongnan minzu xueyuan xuebao
        (Journal of the Central-South Nationalities Institute)
Zhongyang minzu Xxeyuan xuebao (Journal of the Central Nationalities Institute)

Index

About the Author

Thomas Heberer, born in 1947 in Offenbach in the Federal Republic of Germany, is an anthropologist, sinologist, and political scientist; he teaches the politics and economics of China at the University of Duisburg. He lived and worked in China from 1977 to 1981, when he visited numerous minority regions, in some cases for extended periods. Between 1982 and 1988, he revisited several of those regions.